THE LAODICEAN MESSAGE

CHRIST'S URGENT COUNSEL TO A LUKEWARM CHURCH IN THE LAST DAYS

E H SEQUEIRA

I would like to dedicate this book to my wife, Jean and my children Jenny & Christopher.

Contents

Acknowledgements — vii

About The Author — ix

1. Introduction — 1

2. Laodicea Is Addressed — 14

3. Laodicea Is Evaluated, Part 1 — 30

4. Laodicea Is Evaluated, Part 2 — 44

5. Laodicea Is Deceived — 59

6. Laodicea Is Counseled — 74

7. Laodicea Is Rebuked — 89

8. Laodicea Must Repent — 105

9. Laodicea Must Open The Door — 122

10. Laodicea Must Overcome — 140

11. Laodicea Is Sealed — 156

12. Laodicea Is Faultless — 173

Acknowledgements

I would thank many people in my life for helping in coming up with this book.

*First and foremost, my wife, **Jean**. She has ever been a great support and encouragement to me. Without her constant help, things would have been tough.*

*My children, **Jenny & Christopeher**, for teaching me love.*

*Elder **Robert J. Wieland**, for his guidance and theological support. His presentations have always been clear & Jesus-centric.*

Church Members at Walla Walla City Church. They have been a great support to the Ministry.

*And mainly, **God**, for His love, grace, mercy & kindness. Without Him, nothing would ever be in its place. He is the very reason for this material. His care demonstrates us this Message, to which He calls us back to Himself.*

About The Author

Pastor E. H. (Jack) Sequeira was born in Nairobi, Kenya. He joined the Seventh-day Adventist Church through evangelism in 1957. Feeling called to the ministry, he rode to England from Nairobi on his motorcycle in 1958 and spent 14 months working as a literature evangelist before enrolling at Newbold College (England). He graduated with a B.A. in theology in 1963. He earned an M.A. in systematic theology at Andrews University (Berrien Springs, Michigan, U.S.A.) in 1965. Pastor Sequeira earned his M.Div. at Andrews University in 1970.

Pastor E. H. Sequeira got married to Jean on New Year's Day, 1964. They served as missionaries for 17 years in Uganda, Kenya, and Ethiopia. He served in various capacities as Bible teacher, departmental director, university chaplain, union ministerial director, and college president.

In 1982, the Sequeiras moved to the United States. Jack served as pastor for the Kuna and Nampa churches in the Idaho Conference, then as senior pastor of the Walla Walla City Church in Washington State. In 1991, he became senior pastor of the Capital Memorial Church in Washington, D.C. Pastor Jack retired in January 2001 but still ministers to others. He has enjoyed a lifetime of preaching and seminar appointments. Jack enjoys the beautiful Pacific Northwest.

Jack and Jean have two children. Jenny (born in Uganda), was a Peace Corps Volunteer in The Gambia. Christopher (born in Kenya) is married to Nenette.

Jack and Jean live in Oregon and began JackSequeira.org in 2002 to share the Good News of the Gospel and give hope to God's children everywhere.

CHAPTER ONE

Introduction

You will notice that our study this time is an introduction. I want to leave a foundation today, and the first thing I would like to say about this subject is the importance of the study. First of all, the book of Revelation is a prophetic book; in fact, it compliments Daniel in dealing with last day events. A lot of the symbols of Revelation are from Daniel. So when you hear or read about "Babylon, the great city that is fallen," it is linked with the history of the city of Babylon that fell and is mentioned in Daniel.

Now I would like you to turn to Revelation 1, and there are two statements there that I want you to notice as we tackle this subject. Revelation 1, and in verse 1 we are told that this book is:

The revelation of Jesus Christ, which God gave him...

So God gave a revelation to Christ:

...to show his servants [i.e., His church] *what must soon take place.*

So this is a prophetic book; it's known as the Apocalypse, because it's dealing with last day events, just like Daniel. And in verse 3 a statement is made that we need to take note of:

Blessed is the one who [number one] *reads the words of this prophecy, and blessed are those who* [number two] *hear it and* [number three] *take to heart what is written in it, because the time is near.*

In other words, this book is dealing with last day events. So it is an important subject that we are covering; we are dealing with only one aspect of the book of Revelation: the Laodicean message.

Now I want you to look at some Ellen G. White comments and you will notice that the Laodicean message is vitally connected with the doctrine of Righteousness by Faith. Look at the statement found in 7BC 964:

"The Laodicean message has been sounding, take this message in all its phases and sound it forth to the people wherever providence opens the way. Justification by faith and the Righteousness of Christ are the themes to be presented to a perishing world."

So she links the Laodicean message with Justification by faith and the Righteousness of Christ. The next statement, of course, reminds us that in a special way this message is applicable to us [7BC 961]:

"The message to the Laodicean church is highly applicable to us as a people. It has been placed before us for a long time but has not been heeded as it should have been. When the work of repentance is earnest and deep, the individual members of the church will buy the rich goods of heaven" [the three goods that have been offered to us in the counsel to Laodicea].

Now I want you to notice that:

1. The message to Laodicea is the doctrine of Justification by faith, Christ our Righteousness, which should "be presented to the perishing world." That is why I want to make this a Biblical study, because when you preach to the world you cannot use Ellen G. White quotes, you have to use your Bible. So I'm going to quote from the Bible, but I want you to notice that Ellen G. White is in perfect harmony with what the Bible teaches concerning these subjects.

2. I want you to notice that in a special way she applies this message to us as Adventists; we shall see more of that as we go along. But it also applies to other Christian folks. I believe it has a strong application to the Charismatic movement, and I will touch on it.

But let us, first of all, look at two very important rules of interpretation, because we've got to go Biblically. These are rules we've already touched on when we dealt with Daniel, but I'm going to review it in case some of you didn't see it.

Both Daniel and Revelation are prophetic books that deal with last day events. They are prophetic books that personally are concerned — that focus on — the last day events. As I mentioned before, and I'm going to repeat it, there are four schools of thought concerning how to interpret both these books. We as a church uphold what is known as the "Historicist" position. This is the position that was promoted by the Reformation; so we are of the Reformation line, in terms of interpreting Daniel and Revelation. The other two are "Preterist" and "Futurist," and then there's a third one called "Idealist." Now let me explain each one of them quickly. Let's start with the Historicist.

The Reformers believed that both Daniel and Revelation were books that revealed the history of the world and the Christian church beginning at the time of the writers, i.e., with Daniel, about 600 years before Christ, and with John, about 100 years after Christ. They begin there and they give a continuous account of history, ending with the last day events.

If you follow this school, this line of thought, it interprets the little horn of Daniel and the Antichrist of Revelation as being the Papacy and the fulfilment of these two symbols.

Now you can imagine that the Roman Catholic church did not like this. So how did they counteract this interpretation? They came up with two different schools of thought. The Preterist teaches that all the prophecies of Revelation and Daniel were fulfilled within a short period of time of the writers.

For example, by the second century B.C., all the prophecies of Daniel were fulfilled. By the third century A.D., all the prophecies of Revelation were fulfilled. Which means that the papacy was not included in the prophecies; so the Preterist view helped the Catholic Church to escape from being identified with the Little Horn and the Antichrist.

The Futurist, which is also a Roman Catholic interpretation of the prophecies, says that some of the prophecies were fulfilled in Daniel's and John's time, and others will be fulfilled at the end of church history, and in between that time there is a gap. And, of course, that in-between period is the history of the Roman Catholic church; that is not included, they say.

Now, I can understand the Roman Catholics trying to use these two schools of interpretation to defend themselves. But the tragedy is that gradually the Protestant churches have accepted these views, so that today there is no denomination that upholds the Historicist view except the Seventh-day Adventist Church. We are the only ones, as a denomination, that upholds the Historicist interpretation of Daniel and Revelation.

Most Protestants now take the Futurist and Preterist interpretation. And this gap theory, which includes, for instance, the 70 weeks, they say 69 weeks were fulfilled in Daniel's time, the 70th week will be fulfilled at the end of time, and there's a gap. Those who believe in the rapture teach that, the Dispensationalists teach that. So we are kind of unique. But if you look at these two books, you will see that they are historical. The Historicist is a very clear approach.

I would like to say a thing about the idealistic view. It believes that the prophecies of Daniel and Revelation are not prophecies; they're simply symbols revealing spiritual truths. Now this view is held by the liberal theologians; but there are now conservative Christians, including Adventists, who are beginning to follow this. One of them, of course, is Desmond Ford. His concept of the Apocalysmatic principle is based on this view. I am reading a statement from his magazine that had a series of studies on Revelation. Ford believed that the coming of Christ could have taken place at any time, any time during the New Testament time onwards. So he makes this statement:

"The fact that Christ could have returned in John's generation means that John's books sets forth certain basic events only. *[And he's dealing with the book of Revelation.]* The major themes of

Revelation are the Judgement, and Second Advent, and the Great Tribulation, and warning message before the Advent."

"Therefore the book necessarily concentrates on broad themes such as witnessing, persecutions, reformatory judgments, and warnings, the final outpouring of divine wrath prior to the restoration of all things. To search for prediction of specific minor and local events in history is to miss the significance of the whole."

What he's saying is this: that the prophecies of Revelation do not apply specifically to any point of history. They have been repeated many times. During John's day they were repeated, during history they were repeated, and, in our day, in a greater sense, they will be repeated. Therefore, he says, the book of Revelation is not pinpointing certain events that will take place in history. Really what this does is water down the books of Daniel and Revelation. It gives it just general ideas, general themes that will repeat themselves many times. There are many Adventists who are beginning to accept this.

I believe, folks, that the Historicist approach, which the Reformers were proclaiming, was the right approach, and this is the approach that I am going to take in dealing with the book of Revelation.

Now this brings me to the second principle, and it's called "the principle of recapitulation" or "parallelism." Both Daniel and Revelation repeat the histories of the world over and over again; there are parallel passages. For example, Daniel 2, 7, 8, 9, 11, and 12 are parallel passages. They are repeating the very same history but they are approaching it from different angles.

Now the book of Revelation is doing the same thing, except it comes from the angle of sevens. You have the message of the seven churches, you have the seven seals, you have the seven trumpets. They are all dealing with the same period of time but each message is dealing with a different issue.

In other words, the seven churches, the seven seals, the seven trumpets, are covering the same periods of time but from different angles. Now we are going to look in this study only at the seven churches to get the context, because the first thing we need to look at is the context. What is God trying to bring across in the messages to the seven churches?

If you look at the messages to the seven churches, you will find that there is a common thread all through the seven churches' messages. So please look at them in your Bible; we'll start with Revelation 2:1:

To the angel of the church in Ephesus write: These are the words of him who holds the seven stars in his right hand and walks among the seven golden lampstands:...

The first church is Ephesus. Now the common thread is a phrase that is repeated for every church. Verse 2a, what does He say to the Ephesus church?

I know your deeds, your hard work and your perseverance....

Look at verse nine, Smyrna. What does He say to Smyrna? Verse 9a:

I know your afflictions and your poverty....

This phrase, "I know your deeds," (or something similar) is repeated for every church.

Look at verse 13, Pergamum:

I know where you live....

Verse 19a, Thyatira:

I know your deeds, your love and faith, your service and perseverance....

Then chapter 3:1, He's talking to Sardis, and in the last part of that verse He says,

...I know your deeds....

And then Philadelphia in chapter 3, in verse 8 He says:

I know your deeds....

And, of course Laodicea, is the same thing. In verse 15 of chapter 3 He says:

I know your deeds....

So what is Jesus doing in the messages to the seven churches? He is giving us an evaluation of our spiritual condition. You see, God judges the churches, He judges individuals, by their works. Our works tell us what our spiritual condition is. I want to give you several texts to show you that this is a clear teaching of the Bible.

So the messages to the seven churches are God's evaluation of the Christian church beginning with John right up to the last generation of Christians. And, of course, Laodicea is the seventh church, which is dealing with us, the last generation of Christians, which is what I want to look at.

Let me look at some of the passages that will help you to see that our works tell us what our spiritual condition is. For example, look at Matthew 5:14. What does God say to the disciples? In verse 14a, He says:

You are the light of the world....

In other words, you are My witnesses. Christ is the light but you are to represent Me. Now look at verse 16:

In the same way, let your light shine before men, that they may see your good deeds and praise your Father in heaven.

Let your light so shine that men may see what? How do we reveal Christ, by what? By works. And by these we glorify Who? Our Father in heaven.

So our works reveal what kind of people we are. Let me give you another example: in Matthew 25, when Jesus comes He will divide the world into two camps, the sheep and the goats. Now please, nobody is saved by their works. But what does Jesus say to them? "I was hungry and you..." what? Matthew 25:34-36:

"Then the King will say to those on his right, 'Come, you who are blessed by my Father; take your inheritance, the kingdom prepared for you since the creation of the world. For I was hungry and you gave me something to eat, I was thirsty and you gave me something to drink, I was a stranger and you invited me in, I needed clothes and you clothed me, I was sick and you looked after me, I was in prison and you came to visit me.'"

Justification by Faith always bears fruit. And the fruit is feeding the hungry.

You will find this in Matthew 25:34-36. He's using works as evidence that they had accepted His righteousness. At the same time, He uses works to prove those who had rejected Him. And He will say [Matthew 25:41-43]:

"Then he will say to those on his left, 'Depart from me, you who are cursed, into the eternal fire prepared for the devil and his angels. For I was hungry and you gave me nothing to eat, I was thirsty and you gave me nothing to drink, I was a stranger and you did not invite me in, I needed clothes and you did not clothe me, I was sick and in prison and you did not look after me.'"

"I was hungry and you did not feed Me."

I want to give you another example. Turn now to the gospel of John, chapter five. I want you to notice that Jesus used His works to prove that He came from the Father, from God. Look at John 5:36:

"I have testimony weightier than that of John. For the very work that the Father has given me to finish, and which I am doing, testifies that the Father has sent me.

The same thing happens in chapter 14. In chapter 14 of John, Philip says to Jesus [John 14:8]:

Philip said, "Lord, show us the Father and that will be enough for us."

What did Jesus say? Verse 9:

Jesus answered: "Don't you know me, Philip, even after I have been among you such a long time? Anyone who has seen me has seen the Father. How can you say, 'Show us the Father'?"

"He who has seen Me has seen the Father."

I want you to notice verses 10 and 11:

"Don't you believe that I am in the Father, and that the Father is in me? The words I say to you are not just my own. Rather, it is the Father, living in me, who is doing his work. Believe me when I say that I am in the Father and the Father is in me; or at least believe on the evidence of the miracles themselves."

"If you don't believe My words, believe My WORKS. For the works I do are not Mine but the Father Who dwells in Me — He is the One that is doing the works."

So verse 10 and 11 say: "Believe Me for My works' sake."

And, by the way, if you read verse 12, what does Jesus say?

I tell you the truth, anyone who has faith in me will do what I have been doing. He will do even greater things than these, because I am going to the Father.

I want to give you two more examples: one is James 2. Is James teaching Justification by Works? It appears so on the surface, but if you read James 2 very carefully, what He's defending is that genuine justification by faith will always produce works. That is what He's dealing with.

Does Paul agree with Him? Yes. How is our faith witnessed? Not by our words, folks. The world doesn't want you to shout and scream and lift up your hands and say, "Praise the Lord, I am saved!" They don't want that. They want to see Christ in you.

James 2:18a:

But someone will say, "You have faith; I have deeds."

Are these two different things? James says no [18b]:

Show me your faith without deeds, and I will show you my faith by what I do.

Then he goes on to say in verse 19

You believe that there is one God. Good! Even the demons believe that — and shudder.

So what is the conclusion? Verse 20:

You foolish man, do you want evidence that faith without deeds is useless?

Genuine justification by faith always produces works.

So when Jesus says, "I know thy works," He's simply saying, "I'm evaluating you. Are your works good; are your works bad; what is your condition?"

So God judges us by our works. One more text: 1 Peter 2:12:

Live such good lives among the pagans that, though they accuse you of doing wrong, they may see your good deeds and glorify God on the day he visits us.

There Peter tells us that the world may persecute you, not because you have done bad, but because you have done good. But in the judgment, they will admit, they will confess, that your works were not evil. They will have to confess, "Yes, we were wrong in persecuting you."

In concluding our introduction, I want to give you the pattern of the messages. I have already explained to you that the common thread that goes through these messages to the seven churches is "I know your works," which means that God or Christ is evaluating the Christian church at different periods of church history. And we are going to see how Christ evaluates the Christian church in these last days. Or, to be more precise, "How does God evaluate the Adventist church, which is part of the last-day generation of Christians?" How does He evaluate us? According to our works. That is what we are going to study Biblically.

I want to give you the pattern. There are **four** basic terms that are used in all the churches, and I want to give these to you:

1. **Commendation**. He points out the good points of every church in each period, the good points, what He commends.
2. **Reproofs**. Then He has the reproofs. In other words, judging by our works, He says, "This is the good thing about you; this is the bad thing about you."
3. **Counsel**. Then He counsels. God never rebukes us without giving us counsel. In other words, for every problem that the churches face, there is a remedy, there is a counsel.
4. **Promise**. The counsel is followed by a promise. In other words, if you accept the counsel and follow it, there is a promise.

Now I would like to mention something about these four things. Of the seven churches mentioned, there are two that have no reproofs. Those are Smyrna and Philadelphia. Because Philadelphia has no reproofs, there are many who are saying today that Laodicea has to go back to the Philadelphian condition before Christ can come. I am not going to go into that issue, because, you know, it's a theological issue.

I will say this much, that there is reproof for the Laodicean church, but there is something at which you may be surprised. There are two churches that have no commendation, and one of them is the Laodicean church. God had no commendation for us. And that is something that we need to know. In view of this I would like to read you a quotation here by Ellen G. White [3T 252]:

The message to the church of the Laodiceans is a startling denunciation and it is applicable to the people of God at the present time.

You mean to say that here is a church that has present truth and God has no commendation? Isn't that a startling denunciation? And so we're going to see why. Why is it that we have no commendation from Christ? Here is a church that claims to have the truth, here is a church that claims to be the best church, and the rest of them...you know, sometimes we call them Philistines. And yet what does Christ say? "I have nothing good to say about you."

So we must take this very seriously. Where have we gone wrong? What is our problem? We're going to look at it Biblically. This brings me to our conclusion which is dealing with this. The book of Revelation is full of symbols; we must not use our dictionary, or our culture, to interpret the symbols. We need to go to Scripture. So when Christ says to us, "You are not hot, you are not cold, you are lukewarm," we must not give it the modern application of complacency. We need to go to the Bible and say, "What does the Bible mean by 'hot, cold, and lukewarm'?" We need to do that.

So please remember that the book of Revelation is highly symbolic. Therefore, it is like hidden treasure; we have to dig to find out what these symbols represent.

For example, for each Church that is addressed, Christ gives Himself a very special name, and the name that He gives Himself is connected with the message for the Church. Look at the name He gives Himself for us, the Laodiceans. What does He say about Himself concerning us? Look at Revelation 3:14:

To the angel of the church in Laodicea write: These are the words of the Amen, the faithful and true witness, the ruler of God's creation.

Christ is the "Amen." What does He mean by that? He's using it as a noun. He is the "Amen"; He is "the Faithful and True Witness"; and He is the "ruler of God's creation." Now why does He give

Himself these three titles? That is our next study, which will be: "Laodicea is Addressed."

Another question I want to present to you: To whom is the message addressed — to the Church or to somebody else? Look at verse 14:

To the angel of the church in Laodicea....

Who is the Angel of the Church? I want you to wrestle with the symbols. Who is the Angel of Laodicea? What did Jesus mean? Why did He call Himself the "Amen"? The word "amen" means "truth." Why does Jesus call Himself "The Truth"? Why? Ask yourself these questions. I won't give you answers now, because we're going to go on slowly, step by step. All I want you to do is to wrestle with this passage. Don't gloss over this message. We are going to take several studies on just each verse. We'll continue verse by verse. This time we have done the introduction; next our study will be, "Laodicea is Addressed."

I want you to look at verse 14, just Revelation 3:14:

To the angel of the church in Laodicea write: These are the words of the Amen, the faithful and true witness, the ruler of God's creation.

There are two questions I want you to answer regarding verse 14:

1. Who is addressed in verse 14? That means you have to discover who the angel represents. And if you discover the answer from Ellen G. White, that's not enough; you need to go to Scripture. I want you to defend your position from Scripture. That's what the Spirit of Prophecy is for: "She's a lesser light to lead us to the greater light." And we must find out what the greater light says.

2. Who is the One Who is doing the addressing? And why does He call Himself "the Amen," the "true Witness," and "the ruler of God's creation"? Why does He give Himself these three titles? What relationship do these three titles have to do with the message? That is what we will deal with in our next study.

Remember that we are dealing with God's evaluation of the last generation of Christians, and in a very specific way we are dealing with God's evaluation of the Seventh-day Adventist Church. Is it a good evaluation or bad? Is there any commendation? No. Is there any reproof? Yes, I'm afraid so. Does it apply only to a few members, or does it apply to the body? Who is Christ addressing? Just the few who don't come to church, or does it include you? Does it include me?

That is what we need to wrestle with, folks. And you will see, as we go along, that this message that we are dealing with is vitally connected with the message that God brought to this Church in 1888, the message of Righteousness by Faith. And you will see why from the Bible. Ellen G. White makes it clear, but we will see why.

God bless us that we will study this message prayerfully. As you read it, please apply that message to yourself. I will apply it to myself, especially when I look at the word, "angel." It applies to me more than you, folks. But we will see why God addresses it to the angel when He comes to the seven churches.

But you will notice in the introduction, God says to John, "Take these messages and give it to *the churches*." So it does involve the churches, but it begins with the angel. So this is not something that applies to a few members in the church, the backsliders and the cold; it applies to the body of Christ, folks, from the top to the last member.

God bless us as we study this message.

CHAPTER TWO

LAODICEA IS ADDRESSED

Revelation 3:14:

To the angel of the church in Laodicea write: These are the words of the Amen, the faithful and true witness, the ruler of God's creation.

The messages to the seven churches are Christ's evaluation of the spiritual condition of the Christian church during the different periods of church history, because the common thread that goes through all the seven messages is, "I know thy works." And when God looks at our works, He's evaluating us in terms of our spiritual condition. Jesus Himself said, "By their fruits ye shall know them."

Okay, the second thing that we discovered, and this is mainly from Ellen G. White's writings, that while the Laodicean message applies to the Christians of the last generation, it has a special application to us as a people. She clearly points out that the message of the Laodicean church applies, or is highly applicable to us. For example, look at the following quote:

I was shown that the testimony to the Laodiceans applies to God's people at the present time, and the reason it has not accomplished a greater work is because of the hardness of their hearts. [1T 186]

Now that's quite a strong statement.

This is why we need, as a people, to look at this message. We're going to do it Biblically, but these are supplementary helps for our study.

In this study, I want to look at verse 14, "Laodicea is Addressed." This verse is divided into two parts. The first part is dealing with the one who is addressed, and the second half is dealing with the One Who is addressing. Let's read the verse first and then we will look at it in greater detail:

To the angel of the church in Laodicea write: These are the words of the Amen, the faithful and true witness, the ruler of God's creation.

If you turn your Bible to chapter one of Revelation, you will notice that, according to verse 11, the messages to the seven churches are to go to the churches themselves. This is Christ speaking to John, who was in the Spirit on the Lord's day. Revelation 1:8-11:

"I am the Alpha and the Omega," says the Lord God, "who is, and who was, and who is to come, the Almighty."

I, John, your brother and companion in the suffering and kingdom and patient endurance that are ours in Jesus, was on the island of Patmos because of the word of God and the testimony of Jesus. On the Lord's Day I was in the Spirit, and I heard behind me a loud voice like a trumpet, which said: "Write on a scroll what you see and send it to the seven churches: to Ephesus, Smyrna, Pergamum, Thyatira, Sardis, Philadelphia, and Laodicea."

Now, of course I believe that God had a message for the local churches that are mentioned here, but since Revelation, as we saw in the last study, is a prophetic book, it has an application prophetically, and we have seen that it goes over seven periods. These seven churches represent seven periods of the Christian church.

But when you look at verse 14 of chapter 3, which we just read, the Laodicean message is addressed not to the church, but to the Angel of the church. And last study I asked you the question, "Who is the Angel?"

To understand the Angel, let's go back to chapter one and let's look at the introduction to the messages to the seven churches. Revelation 1:12-16:

I turned around to see the voice that was speaking to me. And when I turned I saw seven golden lampstands, and among the lampstands was someone "like a son of man," dressed in a robe reaching down to his feet and with a golden sash around his chest. His head and hair were white like wool, as white as snow, and his eyes were like blazing fire. His feet were like bronze glowing in a furnace, and his voice was like the sound of rushing waters. In his right hand he held seven stars, and out of his mouth came a sharp double-edged sword. His face was like the sun shining in all its brilliance.

Here is John, in the Spirit, on the Lord's day. He hears a voice, that's the voice of Jesus Christ, and those of you who have the red edition Bible will notice it's in red. Then in verse 12 he turns around to see the voice that spoke with him and, being turned, the first thing he sees is seven golden candlesticks.

In verse 13, in the midst of the seven candlesticks, he sees One "like the Son of Man." Now that phrase, "the Son of Man," was the most common phrase used by Jesus Christ regarding Himself. Remember, He asked the disciples on one occasion, "Who do men say the Son of Man is?" And then He said to the disciples, "Who do you say the Son of Man is?" It was a most common phrase, which is the phrase Christ used to identify Himself with us. Please notice that the Son is in capital, therefore, it refers to Christ.

Here is John; he turns around; he sees seven candlesticks. In the midst of those candlesticks, he sees the Son of Man, which is Christ, clothed with a garment down to the foot, and so on. Then you have a description of Jesus Christ in symbolic terms. Folks, these are not literal terms, because you look at verse 14:

And his eyes were like blazing fire.

Well, these are all symbols.

But the verse I want you to look at is verse 16, we looked at verse 12, now verse 16. After describing Christ, and what He looked like in the vision, in verse 16 it says:

In his right hand he [the Son of Man, i.e., Christ] *held seven stars, and out of his mouth came a sharp double-edged sword. His face was like the sun shining in all its brilliance.*

And, by the way, in Hebrews 4:12 the Bible, the Word of God, is defined as a two-edged sword:

For the word of God is living and active. Sharper than any double-edged sword, it penetrates even to dividing soul and spirit, joints and marrow; it judges the thoughts and attitudes of the heart.

But now, there are two things I want you to know in this illustration here, this is what John sees. The first thing he sees is seven candlesticks. And the second thing I want you to notice is verse 16, "He held in His right hand seven stars."

The reason I want you to notice these two things is because these are the two symbols that are explained; and the explanation is found in verse 20:

The mystery of the seven stars that you saw in my right hand and of the seven golden lampstands is this: The seven stars are the angels of the seven churches, and the seven lampstands are the seven churches.

This is Christ explaining these two symbols because they are important.

The candlesticks, therefore, represent the churches themselves, which is a fitting symbol. Turn to Matthew 5. Here again is Jesus talking and please notice what He says about the church, the believers. He's talking about the disciples. This is the Sermon on the Mount. He has just given the Beatitudes, which are the commandments of the Christian church. If you look at these beatitudes you will notice that they very closely relate to what Christ wants the church to be like, the believers to be like.

I want you to notice two verses. First, Matthew 5:14a:

You are the light of the world....

He's talking to the Christians and He is saying, "You are the candlesticks, the lampstands of the world."

I want you to notice something that is very important. You will not notice this in an English Bible, so I'm going to explain it to you, because this is a lot more obvious in the Greek. The "you" is in the plural form. The word "light" is in the singular. Therefore, the "you" represents the church members, all of us; but the "light" represents Who, if it's singular?

Second, John 1:9:

The true light that gives light to every man was coming into the world.

Who is the light of the world? Is it the church, or is it Christ? Jesus said (John 9:5):

...I am the light of the world.

You can read, also, John 1:7-8 [this is talking about John the Baptist]:

He came as a witness to testify concerning that light, so that through him all men might believe. He himself was not the light; he came only as a witness to the light.

But I would like you to look at John 1:12:

Yet to all who received him, to those who believed in his name, he gave the right to become children of God....

Going back to Matthew 5:14, the church is to reflect Whose light? Christ's light. The church is to represent Christ. The world needs to see Christ in the church. Keep this in mind, because when you come to the Laodicean message, you will realize why the church has failed to be the light of the world.

So the church is the light. How does the church reveal Christ? Look at Matthew 5:14-16:

You [i.e., Christians] are the light of the world. A city on a hill cannot be hidden. Neither do people light a lamp and put it under a bowl. Instead they put it on its stand, and it gives light to everyone in the house. In the same way, let your light shine before men, that they may see your good deeds and praise your Father in heaven.

Why do we light a candle? That we may see, to get light. But what do we do? We put it on a candlestick. Now who does the candlestick represent? The church. But God wants that light to go beyond that house, so in verse 16 I read, "Let your light shine before men, that they may see your good deeds and praise your Father in heaven." 'I know your works,' says Jesus. "Let them see your good works and glorify your Father which is in heaven."

Now doesn't Laodicea have good works? Is she not doing good works? Well, we'll come to that in the next study. But what I want you to notice is that the church is the candlestick.

But the Laodicean message is addressed to the "Angel." Who is the angel? What does the word, "angel" mean? "Messenger." Listen to how the Bible describes an angel. Turn to Hebrews 1, and there we have a little help describing in what sense the angels are messengers. Hebrews 1:13-14:

To which of the angels did God ever say, "Sit at my right hand until I make your enemies a footstool for your feet"? Are not all angels ministering spirits sent to serve those who will inherit salvation?

So the angels are ministering spirits. When we use the angels as a symbol, then they refer to those who are spiritual leaders of the church. Let me give you a couple of statements. If you read your Living Bible, which is a paraphrase Bible, you will notice that the Living Bible does not use the word, "angel," but uses the word, "leader": "To the leader of the church of Laodicea."

The Pulpit Commentary interprets the word "angel" as the churches' "chief officers." So it includes Sabbath School teachers and the officers of the church, the elders, but primarily it refers to the ministers and those who are in charge of the spiritual condition of the church.

Please remember that when we use angels as symbols, when they are referred to ministering spirits, the question is, "Are they true ministers or are they false ministers?"

I want you quickly to look at the following quotation, and this may add some little light. You will notice that Ellen G. White agrees with Scripture. This is taken from *Gospel Workers,* pages 13 and 14:

God's ministers are symbolized by seven stars, which He Who is the First and the Last [Christ] has under His special care and protection. The sweet influences that are to be abundant in the church are bound up with these ministers of God, who are to represent the love of Christ. The stars of heaven are under God's control. He fills them with light; He guides and directs their movement. If He did not do this, they would become fallen stars.

That is why we must remember that the spiritual condition of the church is in the hands of the ministers, to a large degree. I want to give you a text to give you an example of this. Turn your Bible to Acts 20, and I want you to notice what Paul does. He's travelling back to Jerusalem from his missionary journey, and he stops at Ephesus, and he's there for a short while. He's not able to preach there, so what does he do? He calls the elders of the church, that's found in 20:17, and from Miletus, or what is now Malta, he sent to Ephesus and called the elders of the church. He is in Malta, he sends a message to the elders.

The word "elders" here is the same word that is used for ministers. It's also used for "bishops." That's why we call ordained ministers "elders"; it's because it comes from this word. And when the elders came, listen to what he says. Look at verse 28. He says:

Keep watch over yourselves and all the flock of which the Holy Spirit has made you overseers. Be shepherds of the church of God, which he bought with his own blood.

In other words, "God has given the members in your care."

That is why I believe that one of the primary tasks of the minister is to feed the church. We have placed upon our pastors a lot of burdens. That is why, when I am first given a call to a church, I call the elders, the board members, just like Paul did, and I say, "Look, what kind of minister are you looking for? Do you want an administrator? Then find somebody else. But if you want somebody who will feed you, that's my concern."

Because that's what Paul says: the spiritual condition of the church depends, to a large degree, on the ministers.

Now let me explain the problem. When we accept Christ (except for rare occasions, like Mary Magdalene, she was exceptional), we accept Christ with a selfish motive. Because our nature is selfish.

Even Ellen White says that when you preach to the world in evangelistic efforts and tell them, "There's a heaven to gain, and a hell to shun," what are you appealing to? The egocentric nature.

So when people accept Christ, they do it for a selfish reason — either because they're afraid of punishment or because they want a reward. I'll be frank with you, both my wife and I joined this church out of fear. We were scared about the judgment we'd been told about in the evangelistic efforts. We were 8,000 miles apart, but you know, our evangelistic meetings are about the same everywhere, we have the same 25 studies. We give them different names, but the basic subject is the same.

In fact, we were holding a Revelation Seminar in Tuna, and one of the men who was coming to the meetings said, "You know, I have come to several evangelistic efforts, and you call them different names, some of them you call "Voice of Prophecy," now you call it "Revelation Seminar," but I discovered it's the same stuff."

And I said to him, "You are right. My problem is, why haven't you accepted it?" He'd been to six or seven of them.

"Well," he said, "I felt that this was a study on Revelation, but you are using Revelation as a stepping stone."

I think that this has been the complaint of many people. So the modern Revelation Seminars, the latest ones that are coming out, are more Revelation-oriented than they were before.

But anyway, when we accept Christ, we do it for a selfish reason. By the way, all of the disciples, all 12 of them, accepted Christ for selfish reasons. What were they arguing about, even three years later? Who shall be the greatest. Who were they thinking of? Themselves.

So when a person joins the church through an evangelistic effort, they are what Paul will define in 1 Corinthians 3:1-3 as "carnal Christians" or "babes in Christ":

Brothers, I could not address you as spiritual but as worldly — mere infants in Christ. I gave you milk, not solid food, for you were not yet ready for it. Indeed, you are still not ready. You are still worldly. For since there is jealousy and quarreling among you, are you not worldly? Are you not acting like mere men?

The work of the pastor is to move them from carnality to spirituality. And you do that by feeding; there has to be spiritual growth. If you don't, you will lose. A carnal Christian is a weak Christian, a baby in Christ, and unless you feed them....

Do you know that in Ethiopia, out of every 20 babies, in some regions, 19 die within the first year. And, in a sense, it's a blessing because of overpopulation, because they have 10, 15 kids in each family. But why do they die? Most of them die because of malnutrition. And it is possible for Christians to die, spiritually, because of malnutrition.

What I want to say here, folks, is that there has to be a spiritual growth. And God is speaking to the Laodicean Church and saying, "Look, you ministers, there is something wrong with the church."

The message is to the whole church, because remember, verse 1:11 says so:

"Write on a scroll what you see and send it to the seven churches: to Ephesus, Smyrna, Pergamum, Thyatira, Sardis, Philadelphia, and Laodicea."

But the responsibility of building up the church is with these ministers. So I plead with you to pray for our ministers, that they would feed the flock, so that we will grow up. There is something wrong; what is wrong we will see in the next study, but let's go on. Look at the following quotation:

"These things saith He that holdeth the seven stars in His right hand." These words are spoken to the teachers in the church, those entrusted by God with weighty responsibilities. [RH 05-26-03]

So who is Christ addressing the message to? To the ministers, so that he or she may realize that there is something wrong with the church. What is wrong? We will discover that in the next study.

Let's go back now to Revelation 3. We have so far addressed ourselves only to the one that is addressed. So God is not speaking to certain individuals in the church; He's speaking to the whole church through the ministers. Because, you see, the spiritual condition of the church will never rise up higher than the ministers. There might be individuals who will be spiritually superior to the ministers, but the general spiritual condition of the church is in direct proportion to the spiritual condition of the ministers. Therefore, this is something that is very serious. The whole church, from the top to the bottom, needs to know this message.

Now let's look at the second half, which is also important. Who is addressing the ministers? Revelation 3:14 says:

To the angel of the church in Laodicea write: These are the words of the Amen, the faithful and true witness, the ruler of God's creation.

The word "Amen" here is used as a proper noun. The word itself, as I touched on previously, actually means, "so be it." Or it can mean, "the truth." The word, "amen" is sometimes translated as "truth"; it can mean "what is being said is the truth."

Now the actual meaning of the word, "Amen," here, is given by Christ Himself. The second phrase after "amen," the next phrase, is the definition of "amen." So Jesus is saying, "This is the Amen, the Truth speaking, the Faithful and True Witness."

Now, you will discover that in every one of the seven messages, Jesus gives Himself a special title, and the title He gives Himself is in harmony with the needs of the church itself. In other words, the title that Christ gives Himself in the Laodicean message, is based on the needs of the Laodicean church and it's connected with the Laodicean message. There are two things that are said about Christ in this second half of verse 14. Number one, Christ is called the "Amen, the Faithful and True Witness."

By the way, you may want to look at Isaiah 65:16, for there God calls Himself, "the God of Truth":

Whoever invokes a blessing in the land will do so by the God of truth; he who takes an oath in the land will swear by the God of truth. For the past troubles will be forgotten and hidden from my eyes.

Why does God call Himself the "Amen" here? Why does He call Himself "the True and Faithful Witness"? Because there is a problem. What is the problem? Look at verse 17 (we will not study verse 17 now but I just want you to look at it). If you look at verse 17, you will notice that there are two evaluations of Laodicea. One is Christ's and one is the church's itself. And these two evaluations do not agree. Look at Revelation 3:17:

You say, 'I am rich; I have acquired wealth and do not need a thing.' But you do not realize that you are wretched, pitiful, poor, blind and naked.

Who is the "you" here? To whom is that message addressed? The angel! Remember, who is it addressed to? So "you" here, refers to the angel. "You ministers, you leaders, are saying about your church, that you are rich, and increased with goods, and have need of nothing. You're making glowing reports about yourself, BUT there is a problem. What is that you do not know? That you are really wretched, and miserable, and poor, and blind, and naked."

Who says that we are wretched? Who says that we are miserable? Christ, the true witness. What do we say about ourselves? That we are rich and increased with goods. What does Christ say about ourselves? Do these two evaluations agree? Do they harmonize, or do they disagree? Who is right? That's what He wants us to know.

I want to make it very clear that we are a corporate body. If your hand is sick, the whole body is affected. Is that clear? Let me give you an example. When Daniel prayed in Daniel 9, and he said, "WE have gone wrong." Is that true about Daniel Himself? No. But what did he do? He identified himself with his people. You see, this is my main complaint with off-shoot movements. They look upon the shortcomings of the church, and then they look upon themselves as if they are on the right track. We need to identify ourselves with the mistakes of the church. I can stand up and say, "I am okay, I'm feeding you people." No, folks, I am in it too, because I'm part of the body.

Well, what I'm saying here, folks, is that we have a problem, the same problem that Peter had. I want you quickly to turn to a passage that will help you, and that is Matthew 26:31-35:

Then Jesus told them, "This very night you will all fall away on account of me, for it is written: 'I will strike the shepherd, and the sheep of the flock will be scattered.' But after I have risen, I will go ahead of you into Galilee."

Peter replied, "Even if all fall away on account of you, I never will."

"I tell you the truth," Jesus answered, "this very night, before the rooster crows, you will disown me three times."

But Peter declared, "Even if I have to die with you, I will never disown you." And all the other disciples said the same.

You are familiar with the incident. This is Jesus talking to His disciples. And He said, "All of you will deny Me. You will forsake me."

How did the disciples relate to that statement? And how did especially Peter relate to that statement? I want you to look at the last few verses. Verse 31 says,

"This very night you will all fall away on account of me, for it is written [He's quoting from the Old Testament]: *'I will strike the shepherd, and the sheep of the flock will be scattered.'"*

Well, they denied it. Look at verse 33:

Peter replied, "Even if all fall away on account of you, I never will."

Is he agreeing or disagreeing with Christ? Who was right? Did Peter discover that the easy way or the hard way? Don't you think he would have saved himself a lot of embarrassment and problems if he had said, "Yes, Lord, You know all things."

Look at verses 34-35:

"I tell you the truth," Jesus answered, "this very night, before the rooster crows, you will disown me three times."

But Peter declared, "Even if I have to die with you, I will never disown you." And all the other disciples said the same.

Peter said, "You've got it all wrong, Jesus." And then the disciples joined in. You see, the disciples had the Laodicean problem. They learnt the hard way.

Now what Jesus is saying is, "I am the True Witness. What I'm telling you is the truth. You may not agree with Me, but I'm telling you the truth."

If we don't learn to listen to Christ now, we will have to learn the hard way. Because He says, "If you don't repent I will rebuke you and I will spew you out of My mouth." Boy, that's terrible.

Anyway, let's go on, back to Revelation 3:14:

To the angel of the church in Laodicea write: These are the words of the Amen, the faithful and true witness, the ruler of God's creation.

The King James Version translation of this phrase has caused a lot of problems. I need to touch on it. In that translation, Jesus gives Himself the title, "the Beginning of the creation of God." There are many Christians in the history of the Christian church who have taken this verse, including our pioneers folks — Jones and Waggoner, Prescott, James White — and they have taught that Jesus had a beginning. "He was the First of God's creation." I'm quoting now from Waggoner, in His book, *Christ Our Righteousness*, "But it was so far in the distant past, that to us human beings, it's like eternity."

But Ellen G. White corrected it. In *Desire of Ages* she says:

"In Him was life original, underived, unborrowed."

It was to counteract the Semi-Arian position of our church. We were Arians. Arius was one of the church leaders in the early church who said that Christ had a beginning. So I need to explain this. The word "beginning" in the Greek does not mean "the beginning" in the sense of "starting." It means, "the source" or "the origin" or "the chief cause." So what Christ is saying here is, "I am the Source of all creation."

And this is the clear teaching of the New Testament. John 1:3 says:

Through him all things were made; without him nothing was made that has been made.

I'll give you several texts. 1 Corinthians 8:6 talks about Christ as a Creator:

...Yet for us there is but one God, the Father, from whom all things came and for whom we live; and there is but one Lord, Jesus Christ, through whom all things came and through whom we live.

Ephesians 3:9:

...And to make plain to everyone the administration of this mystery, which for ages past was kept hidden in God, who created all things.

Also, Colossians 1:16-17:

For by him all things were created: things in heaven and on earth, visible and invisible, whether thrones or powers or rulers or authorities; all things were created by him and for him. He is before all things, and in him all things hold together.

What Christ is saying here, is that "I am not only the True Witness, but I am the Source of all creation, and I can change you, if you only allow Me. I can create in you a new heart, I can make you a new person, only if you will repent, and accept my evaluation of you."

So He is not only saying, "I am the True Witness" but "I am also the solution to your problem." That's why He gives Himself two titles: "I am the True Witness, because you need to know your true condition, which is subconscious or unconscious, you are not aware of it." And we will see why we are not aware of it next study. But number two, "I have a solution to your problem. I am the Source of creation. Everything was made by Me and I can give you a new heart."

In other words, He wants to fulfill in us the New Covenant promise. By the way, I would like to give you a couple of verses which tell you about the New Covenant promise. He made this promise to the Jews first. But the Jews rejected Him. So what did Christ do with the Jews as a nation, not as individuals, but as a nation, what did He do? He said on the triumphal entry to Jerusalem when He wept with tears (Matthew 23:37-38):

O Jerusalem, Jerusalem, you who kill the prophets and stone those sent to you, how often I have longed to gather your children together, as a hen gathers her chicks under her wings, but you were not willing. Look, your house is left to you desolate.

In other words, "I'm going to spew you out of my mouth as a nation. And I will turn to the Gentiles, the Christian church."

But He made them a promise. He did not fulfill that promise to the Jews because they refused Jesus Christ. He's making the same promise to us today, because the same promise is repeated in Hebrews 8. But the promise is found in Ezekiel — also in Jeremiah — but Ezekiel is what I want to look at. Ezekiel 11:19-20:

I will give them an undivided heart and put a new spirit in them; I will remove from them their heart of stone and give them a heart of flesh. Then they will follow my decrees and be careful to keep my laws. They will be my people, and I will be their God.

Also Ezekiel 36:26-27:

I will give you a new heart and put a new spirit in you; I will remove from you your heart of stone and give you a heart of flesh. And I will put my Spirit in you and move you to follow my decrees and be careful to keep my laws.

And you will notice that these promises are repeated in Hebrews 8:10-13:

"This is the covenant I will make with the house of Israel after that time, declares the Lord. I will put my laws in their minds and write them on their hearts. I will be their God, and they will be my people. No longer will a man teach his neighbor, or a man his brother, saying, 'Know the Lord,' because they will all know me, from the least of them to the greatest. For I will forgive their wickedness and will remember their sins no more."

By calling this covenant "new," he has made the first one obsolete; and what is obsolete and aging will soon disappear.

And what is our conclusion? Christ is addressing not a few people in the church, He's addressing the whole church, through its leadership. This is not a problem of some of the members, this is a problem of the body of Christ, the last generation of Christians, and especially to us.

And His evaluation of us is negative, yet it is true, folks; it is true. The question is, "Are we willing to accept His evaluation, no matter how painful it is?" It's very painful, folks, when somebody says to us that, "You are wretched, miserable, poor, blind, and naked." As the church that claims to have the truth, it's very painful. But we will discover in what sense we are wretched, miserable, poor, and blind.

I want to give you a text that will help you to understand our problem too. Jeremiah 17:9:

The heart is deceitful above all things and beyond cure. Who can understand it?

And, folks, we have been deceived, just as the Jews were deceived. The Jews rejected Christ because they did not accept His verdict about them. We must not do the same thing.

We will look at the evaluation of Laodicea in the next study, and I want you to read very carefully verses 15 and 16. Please remember that the words "hot," "cold," and "lukewarm" are symbols that must be interpreted from Scripture and not from your dictionary.

So you wrestle with these two verses, because when we look at the evaluation, we will have to make a response: is it true, or is it false? If it is true, then we will take the counsel; if it is not true, we will refuse the counsel. So verse 15 and 16 are extremely important. What is our problem; what is it that we do not know; what is it that has deceived us? That is why our next study is extremely important, and I want you to study it carefully yourselves. So may God bless us; as we look at this message, we will see what our problem is.

CHAPTER THREE

Laodicea is Evaluated, Part 1

Revelation 3:15-16:

I know your deeds, that you are neither cold nor hot. I wish you were either one or the other! So, because you are lukewarm – neither hot nor cold – I am about to spit you out of my mouth.

Please turn your Bible to Revelation 3. We are dealing with the Laodicean message; we looked at the introduction, which is verse 14, in the last study. We saw that the One addressing the Laodiceans is Christ Himself. He calls Himself, "The Faithful and True Witness," and we saw why. We also saw that Christ is addressing the "Angel"; please notice that it is in the singular, therefore, He is addressing the corporate leadership and, along with it, the church members.

Today I want to deal with verses 15 and 16. To me, this is the most important section of the Laodicean message. It is so important that I'm not going to rush through it, and I think that we will have to spend at least two studies with it.

I'll tell you why these two verse are important: because a clear understanding of Revelation 3:15-16 is the key to a meaningful study of the whole of the Laodicean message. In other words, everything depends on a correct understanding of what Christ is telling us in verses 15 and 16. Christ is evaluating us in these two verses, and that's the title of this study, "Laodicea is Evaluated."

Then, based on that, are verses 17-21; so we need to have a correct understanding.

I want to go step by step. First of all, I would like to read the two verses. So please follow me in your Bible. Jesus, the True and Faithful Witness, is telling us (Revelation 3:15-16):

I know your deeds, that you are neither cold nor hot. I wish you were either one or the other! So, because you are lukewarm — neither hot nor cold — I am about to spit you out of my mouth.

The key statement in these two verses is: "I know your deeds." What does that mean? First of all, the word "deeds" ("works," in some translations) has to do with behaviour, it has to do with our activities. Now Jesus is not referring here to our denominational or institutional works, like our hospitals, or our schools, or our orphanages, or nursing homes, whatever we do. He is discussing here our spiritual behaviour. And, if our spiritual behaviour is wrong — which it is — then, naturally, our other works will be affected. So it is important that we understand, "How does Christ evaluate our spiritual works?"

The first thing that we need to know about this is that Laodicea is not short of deeds. This makes it very clear: "I know your deeds." So it is not that we don't have deeds; that's not the issue. We have deeds, but there is something wrong with those deeds. It is neither hot, nor cold but it is lukewarm, and lukewarm is a mixture of hot and cold. So that is basically what He is saying. It is not hot, it is not cold, but it is lukewarm.

Now you need to notice that these terms, these symbols — hot, lukewarm, and cold — are used in reference to our works. He says, "I know your deeds." Our deeds are not hot. But our works are lukewarm.

We're still dealing with behaviour here. "You're spiritual behaviour is not hot, it is not cold, but it is lukewarm." You will notice that there are three kinds of works here mentioned. These are symbols; please remember, the book of Revelation is symbolic. Now if you read your New Testament carefully, you will discover that the New Testament describes human behaviour when it talks on a spiritual level, it describes human behaviour in three categories:

1. Works of the flesh,
2. Works of faith,
3. Works of the law.

These are the three categories of works that the New Testament describes: works of the flesh, works of the law, and works of faith. To which of these three do the categories belong? In other words, do "hot" deeds symbolize works of the flesh, works of the law, or works of faith? That is what we need to discover. And we need to discover what cold works belong to. I'm going to start with cold works.

First of all, I want to make a statement and then I will come back to it and show you from the Bible what it represents. I believe that "cold" works represent works of the flesh. Let me describe the word "flesh." When the word "flesh" is used in the New Testament in a spiritual sense, it refers to our carnal, fallen, sinful nature. So when Paul says, "I am carnal, I am fleshly" (that's the Greek word), he means, "I am a fallen man." So "flesh" represents our fallen, sinful nature.

What does "works of the flesh" represent? Please turn your Bible to Galatians 5, where Paul clearly describes "works of the flesh." Let's look at verses 19-21:

The acts of the sinful nature are obvious: sexual immorality, impurity and debauchery; idolatry and witchcraft; hatred, discord, jealousy, fits of rage, selfish ambition, dissensions, factions and envy; drunkenness, orgies, and the like. I warn you, as I did before, that those who live like this will not inherit the kingdom of God.

So if you are to describe the works of the flesh, what would you call it? In one word? Sin! Is that clear? So "works of the flesh" is what kind of behaviour, good or bad? It belongs to which camp? The camp of sin. Now let me give you another example, Romans 7:14. Paul says,

We know that the law is spiritual; but I am unspiritual, sold as a slave to sin.

Then he explains this. But I want you to look at the conclusion, which is the last statement found in verse 25. If you read verses 15-24 you will notice what Paul is saying. For example, look at Romans 7:18:

I know that nothing good lives in me, that is, in my sinful nature. For I have the desire to do what is good, but I cannot carry it out.

In other words, Paul is saying the flesh is incapable of doing good. And he proves this; he says (Romans 7:19-21):

For what I do is not the good I want to do; no, the evil I do not want to do — this I keep on doing. Now if I do what I do not want to do, it is no longer I who do it, but it is sin living in me that does it. So I find this law at work: When I want to do good, evil is right there with me.

"Even if I want to do good, I find that I cannot do it."

But the key text is the last part of verse 25:

Thanks be to God — through Jesus Christ our Lord! So then, I myself in my mind am a slave to God's law, but in the sinful nature a slave to the law of sin.

Now we must put the emphasis on those two words, "I myself." The word translated "I myself" in the Greek is *ego*. But Paul uses two words instead of one, he uses the words *autos ego*, which means, "Left on my own, without the help of the Holy Spirit, on my own, the only thing that I can do is keep the law in the mind, but, in the flesh, I keep sinning.

That's why in Romans 8:7 he says:

The sinful mind [the mind controlled by the flesh] *is hostile to God. It does not submit to God's law, nor can it do so.*

In other words, can the flesh do good things? Outwardly, yes, but, according to the Bible, can the flesh do anything good? No.

Now I want to give you another text that may help you, John 3:6. When Jesus was met by Nicodemus, remember the night visitor? Nicodemus was a Pharisee. By the way, we have a tendency to look at the Pharisees as being bad people. But actually the Pharisees were zealous about keeping the law. If you read Philippians 3:4-6, where

Paul describes himself as a Pharisee, he was zealous regarding the righteousness of the law, he was blameless:

...Though I myself have reasons for such confidence. If anyone else thinks he has reasons to put confidence in the flesh, I have more: circumcised on the eighth day, of the people of Israel, of the tribe of Benjamin, a Hebrew of Hebrews; in regard to the law, a Pharisee; as for zeal, persecuting the church; as for legalistic righteousness, faultless.

A Pharisee is someone who is really trying to do right. But how is he doing it, in whose power? His own power. Keep this in mind, because that is the problem when Jesus is talking to Nicodemus.

In John 3:6, Jesus makes a statement to Nicodemus, he says to him:

Flesh gives birth to flesh, but the Spirit gives birth to spirit.

In other words, the flesh is unchangeable. He's telling Nicodemus: "Your foundation is wrong. You are trying to keep the will of God by your flesh. And the flesh will always remain flesh. You need to be born from above, you need to have another power." So please remember the word "flesh" refers to our sinful nature, and "works of the flesh," as we saw in Galatians 5, are sinful acts.

Why do I identify this with "cold"? Let me give you some texts. Turn first of all to Matthew 24, and look at verse 12. This is Jesus prophesying about the last days, and one of the last things he tells us about the last days, which we're witnessing today, is this (Matthew 24:12):

Because of the increase of wickedness, the love of most will grow cold....

So Jesus identifies cold with sinful acts, with iniquity. And you will find this quite common. In Ephesians 5:11, Paul gives another description of the works of the flesh. He just uses another term, but it means the same thing:

Have nothing to do with the fruitless deeds of darkness, but rather expose them.

What does he say there? How does he describe the works of the flesh? He gives it another term, but it is the same thing, it's synonymous with works of the flesh: "the fruitless deeds of darkness."

In 1 Thessalonians 5:5, you will notice that Paul puts people in two categories. Christians he calls "the children of light" and unbelievers are called the children of "darkness":

You are all sons of the light and sons of the day. We do not belong to the night or to the darkness.

Please remember that, in the Middle East, you have extremes of temperature. In 1980, I gave a series of workers meetings, and the pastors, in appreciation for those workers meetings, took me on a trip. They gave me a free trip to Mount Sinai, where the law was given. I was quite amazed: the daytime was awfully hot — sometimes it reached 112 degrees Fahrenheit — but the nights! I forgot to take warm stuff, because we left in the daytime, but the nights were freezing cold. I had to borrow and do everything, even my sleeping bag was too cold. You have this extreme of temperature.

During the Exodus, because of these extremes in temperature, in the daytime, God was a cloud to keep them cool. Because it's quite cool in Egypt in the shade; it's in the sun that it's hot. In the nighttime, He was a pillar of fire, so He had a miraculous heating system. So the Jews kept warm in the night, and they kept cool in the day, and God was their Protector. He was supplying their needs.

So you can see that cold is identified with works of the flesh. Now go back to Galatians 5. What is the opposite of cold? Hot. And what is the opposite of works of the flesh? Let's look at Galatians 5; because in Galatians 5:16, Paul is making a statement, and the works of the flesh is based on that statement. He says:

So I say, live by the Spirit, and you will not gratify the desires of the sinful nature.

So there are two kinds of walks that are available to the Christian: you can walk in the flesh and you can walk in the Spirit. If you walk in the Spirit, you can overcome the flesh. That's what he's saying. Then, in verses 19-20, he describes the works of the flesh, which are produced by people who walk in the flesh:

The acts of the sinful nature are obvious: sexual immorality, impurity and debauchery; idolatry and witchcraft; hatred, discord, jealousy, fits of rage, selfish ambition, dissensions, factions and envy; drunkenness, orgies, and the like. I warn you, as I did before, that those who live like this will not inherit the kingdom of God.

But in verse 22, which is the opposite — because it begins with the word "but," it means "in contrast" — the fruit of the Spirit is what? Galatians 5:22-23:

But the fruit of the Spirit is love, joy, peace, patience, kindness, goodness, faithfulness, gentleness and self-control. Against such things there is no law.

I would like to show you here that the fruit of the Spirit is synonymous with works of faith. Let me give you an example. Let's start with Jesus Christ, John 14:12:

I tell you the truth, anyone who has faith in me will do what I have been doing. He will do even greater things than these, because I am going to the Father.

"If you have faith, you will do the works of Christ."

What has Christ going to the Father have to do with doing those works? I'll tell you why; because in John 16:7 Jesus said:

But I tell you the truth: It is for your good that I am going away. Unless I go away, the Counselor will not come to you; but if I go, I will send him to you.

"If I don't go to My Father, I will not be able to send you the Holy Spirit."

In other words, when we walk by faith, the Holy Spirit Who dwells in the believer will produce the works of Christ. I want to give you a couple more examples regarding this. Let's look at Titus 3:8:

This is a trustworthy saying. And I want you to stress these things, so that those who have trusted in God may be careful to devote themselves to doing what is good. These things are excellent and profitable for everyone.

These are works of faith, because they who believe will produce these works.

Let me give you another text, and that is 1 Thessalonians 1:3. What is Paul saying here? He's introducing himself, he's writing an introduction to the Thessalonians. He says in verse 3:

We continually remember before our God and Father your work produced by faith, your labor prompted by love, and your endurance inspired by hope in our Lord Jesus Christ.

Another passage is James 2:14-26, where James is saying that genuine faith always produces works. And faith without works is dead. If your faith doesn't produce works, it is because your faith is dead. James 2:14-26:

What good is it, my brothers, if a man claims to have faith but has no deeds? Can such faith save him? Suppose a brother or sister is without clothes and daily food. If one of you says to him, "Go, I wish you well; keep warm and well fed," but does nothing about his physical needs, what good is it? In the same way, faith by itself, if it is not accompanied by action, is dead.

But someone will say, "You have faith; I have deeds." Show me your faith without deeds, and I will show you my faith by what I do.

You believe that there is one God. Good! Even the demons believe that—and shudder.

You foolish man, do you want evidence that faith without deeds is useless? Was not our ancestor Abraham considered righteous for what he did when he offered his son Isaac on the altar? You see that his faith and his actions were working together, and his faith was made complete by what he did. And the scripture was fulfilled that says, "Abraham believed God, and it was credited to him as righteousness," and he was called God's friend. You see that a person is justified by what he does and not by faith alone.

In the same way, was not even Rahab the prostitute considered righteous for what she did when she gave lodging to the spies and sent them off in a different direction? As the body without the spirit is dead, so faith without deeds is dead.

Please remember these first two texts. I gave you Thessalonians because Paul believes in works of faith. He's thanking the Thessalonians for their work of faith. He's telling Titus that those who believe will maintain good works.

Now if "cold" is the works of the flesh, then hot must be works of faith. So we have now identified two kinds of works. But what I want to now is to look at "lukewarm." If "hot" is works of faith, and "cold" is works of the flesh, then "lukewarm" would be what kind of works? What is left? Works of law.

Now I want to give you some texts that define works of faith. While you're looking at it, let me give you an explanation. Please turn to Romans 9:30-32:

What then shall we say? That the Gentiles, who did not pursue righteousness, have obtained it, a righteousness that is by faith; but Israel, who pursued a law of righteousness, has not attained it. Why not? Because they pursued it not by faith but as if it were by works. They stumbled over the "stumbling stone."

Who was that stumbling stone that they stumbled at? Yes, if you read verse 33 you will notice that it applies to Christ; because it says:

As it is written: "See, I lay in Zion a stone that causes men to stumble and a rock that makes them fall, and the one who trusts in him [Jesus Christ] *will never be put to shame."*

We will come to that, because you remember what Jesus, the True Witness, says to Laodicea (Revelation 3:18):

I counsel you to buy from me gold refined in the fire, so you can become rich; and white clothes to wear, so you can cover your shameful nakedness; and salve to put on your eyes, so you can see.

Let me give you another text. I'll give you a couple in Galatians — Galatians 2:16 — and you will notice that Paul uses the phrase "works of the law" ["observing the law" in the NIV translation] more than once:

Know that a man is not justified by observing the law, but by faith in Jesus Christ. So we, too, have put our faith in Christ Jesus that we may be justified by faith in Christ and not by observing the law, because by observing the law no one will be justified.

If you turn to chapter 3, the next chapter, verse 10, we have a very important verse there:

All who rely on observing the law are under a curse, for it is written: "Cursed is everyone who does not continue to do everything written in the Book of the Law."

What did Paul mean by that phrase "observing the law" or "works of the law"? You see, they did not have a word in the Greek language that was equivalent to our English word "legalism." There is no Greek word for legalism. So the expression, the phrase "works of the law" is "legalism." So whenever you read this expression, "works of the law," it's legalism.

How would you define legalism? How would you define "works of the law"? Let me give you a text that will help you, Philippians 3:7-9. Here Paul is telling us what he's giving up in exchange for Christ. I want you to notice the phrase he uses in verse 9:

But whatever was to my profit I now consider loss for the sake of Christ. What is more, I consider everything a loss compared to the surpassing greatness of knowing Christ Jesus my Lord, for whose sake I have lost all things. I consider them rubbish, that I may gain Christ and be found in him, not having a righteousness of my own that comes from the law, but that which is through faith in Christ — the righteousness that comes from God and is by faith.

We have a term in English to define "a righteousness of my own that comes from the law," in other words, works of the law. We have an expression in English, "self-righteousness," that's how we call it in English, righteousness that is produced by self.

I want to show you how self-righteousness, or works of the law, is a mixture of cold and hot. In self-righteousness, who is doing the works, the Spirit or the flesh? So the flesh is doing the works. But the works that the flesh is doing, is it good, or does it resemble the righteousness of the law outwardly? What did the Pharisee pray? Luke 18:11-12:

The Pharisee stood up and prayed about himself: "God, I thank you that I am not like other men — robbers, evildoers, adulterers — or even like this tax collector. I fast twice a week and give a tenth of all I get."

Or in Matthew 19:16-30, look at the young man who came to Jesus:

Now a man came up to Jesus and asked, "Teacher, what good thing must I do to get eternal life?"

"Why do you ask me about what is good?" Jesus replied. "There is only One who is good. If you want to enter life, obey the commandments."

"Which ones?" the man inquired.

Jesus replied, "Do not murder, do not commit adultery, do not steal, do not give false testimony, honor your father and mother,' and 'love your neighbor as yourself."

"All these I have kept," the young man said. "What do I still lack?"

Jesus answered, "If you want to be perfect, go, sell your possessions and give to the poor, and you will have treasure in heaven. Then come, follow me."

When the young man heard this, he went away sad, because he had great wealth.

Then Jesus said to his disciples, "I tell you the truth, it is hard for a rich man to enter the kingdom of heaven. Again I tell you, it is easier for a camel to go through the eye of a needle than for a rich man to enter the kingdom of God."

When the disciples heard this, they were greatly astonished and asked, "Who then can be saved?"

Jesus looked at them and said, "With man this is impossible, but with God all things are possible."

Peter answered him, "We have left everything to follow you! What then will there be for us?"

Jesus said to them, "I tell you the truth, at the renewal of all things, when the Son of Man sits on his glorious throne, you who have followed me will also sit on twelve thrones, judging the twelve tribes of Israel. And everyone who has left houses or brothers or sisters or father or mother or children or fields for my sake will receive a hundred times as much and will inherit eternal life. But many who are first will be last, and many who are last will be first."

Jesus said, "If you want to go to heaven by your works, you must keep the law." And the young man said, "Which law?" And Jesus gave him the six commandments which deal in terms of our relationship with our neighbor. And what did the young man say? "All these things have I kept since I was in primary Sabbath school."

Now what kind of works did the young man do? Works of the law. "Works of the law" means "flesh" trying to produce the righteousness of the law which belongs to the heart. So the source of works of the law is flesh. But the works themselves resemble what? Works of faith or righteousness.

Let me give you an illustration. Do "works of faith" keep the Sabbath? Yes. Do "works of the law" keep the Sabbath? Yes. Here is a Jew who is keeping the Sabbath. The question is not, "Are you keeping the Sabbath?" But, "Is that keeping of the Sabbath works of the law or is it works of faith? That is important. But that I will cover when we do verse 17, when we see why works of the law deceive us.

But the question is the works of the law is not the same as the works of the flesh, because the works of the flesh are sinful acts; the works of the law are not sinful acts. They are righteous acts on the surface, they look good, but they are very deceiving, because outwardly they look good. So please remember that "works of the law" is self-righteousness.

Now I want to turn to the quotations from Ellen G. White. And I want to read three quotations. And I want you to notice how she identifies the Laodicean problem. You notice that she agrees with this exegesis.

Your self-righteousness is nauseating to the Lord Jesus Christ.

"I know your deeds, that thou art neither cold nor hot; I would that thou wert cold or hot. So then because thou art lukewarm, and neither cold nor hot, I will spew thee out of My mouth. Because thou sayest, I am rich, and increased with goods, and have need of nothing; and knowest not that thou art wretched, and miserable, and poor, and blind, and naked: I counsel thee to buy of me gold tried in the fire, that thou mayest be rich; and white raiment, that thou mayest be clothed, and that the shame of thy nakedness do not appear; and anoint thine eyes with eyesalve, that thou mayest see."

These words apply to the churches and to many of those in positions of trust in the work of God. [7BC 962]

So what is our problem? Self-righteousness. Next quotation:

Self-righteousness is not the wedding garment...

In fact, self-righteousness is the garment that one person was wearing, refusing the garment that was offered him. The bridegroom was offering him His garment, he says, "No, my suit is pretty clean. I don't need your suit." And Sister White says:

Self-righteousness is not the wedding garment. A failure to follow the clear light of truth is our fearful danger. The message to the Laodicean church reveals our condition as a people. [RH 12-15-04]

What is our condition? Self-righteousness. Okay, let me give you one more quotation. Here we are told what Christ's opinion is of self-righteousness [SC 44]:

There are those who profess to serve God while they rely upon their own efforts to obey His law...

How would you describe these kind of works — "works of faith" or "works of the law"? Who are they depending on to produce righteousness? They're depending on their own effort.

There are those who profess to serve God while they rely upon their own efforts to obey His law to form a right character and secure salvation. Their hearts are not moved by any deep sense of the love of Christ, but they seek to perform the duties of the Christian life as which God requires of them in order to gain heaven. Such religion is worth nothing!

So you see, Ellen G. White agrees with what we've been studying. Only I am doing it from the Bible because we need to defend our message from the word of God. But I'm giving you these quotations to see that there is perfect harmony.

So here is our problem. Of course, we have not finished our study of these two verses. I'm going to spend another study, but I would like to present one question. If you turn back to Revelation 3:15, the last part, Jesus makes a statement that I want you folks to wrestle with. We'll touch on it next time:

I know your deeds, that you are neither cold nor hot. I wish you were either one or the other!

You mean He wants us to be cold? What did He mean when He said, "I wish you were either cold or hot"? Why did He say that?

There is a statement where God says it will be easier in the judgment for Nineveh than for Israel. Matthew 12:41:

The men of Nineveh will stand up at the judgment with this generation and condemn it; for they repented at the preaching of Jonah, and now one greater than Jonah is here.

When God told Nineveh that "you are wicked," did they agree? Yes. What was Nineveh guilty of — works of the law or works of the flesh? Works of the flesh. Their behaviour was terrible.

When God told Israel that "your works are wrong," did they agree? No. In other words, they were blind to their condition, and we will see when we come to verse 17 why they didn't realize it. But we need to wrestle with WHY Jesus says that, "I wish you were either hot or cold" and, number two, why does He object to self-righteousness?

Let me give you an illustration. If you have a child who is trying his best to please you, are you angry or are you happy? You're happy. But here is a person who is trying to please God with his own efforts, and God is angry. Why? Well, that's for next study.

CHAPTER FOUR

LAODICEA IS EVALUATED, PART 2

What we did in our last study was to look at those three terms or symbols that Jesus used. He said (Revelation 3:15-16):

I know your deeds, that you are neither cold nor hot. I wish you were either one or the other! So, because you are lukewarm — neither hot nor cold — I am about to spit you out of my mouth.

So these symbols — hot, lukewarm, and cold — are linked with this statement. In other words, this is the key statement: "I know your deeds." Your deeds are not hot, your deeds are not cold, your deeds are lukewarm.

These are symbols, and we spent some time in the last study looking at the symbols. We saw that "hot" works are works of faith. There are three kinds of works described in the New Testament. "Works of faith" are works produced by the Holy Spirit Who dwells in you as you walk by faith.

Another expression for works of faith in Galatians 5:22-25 is the "fruit of the Spirit":

But the fruit of the Spirit is love, joy, peace, patience, kindness, goodness, faithfulness, gentleness and self-control. Against such things there is no law. Those who belong to Christ Jesus have crucified the sinful nature with its passions and desires. Since we live by the Spirit, let us keep in step with the Spirit.

So the "fruit of the Spirit" and "works of faith" are synonymous.

We saw also that "works of flesh" is what human nature, which is sinful, does. Works of flesh are sinful acts which we perform because of our sinful nature. Another phrase for works of the flesh is Ephesians 5:11 where Paul calls it, "deeds of darkness."

Have nothing to do with the fruitless deeds of darkness, but rather expose them.

So "deeds of darkness" and "works of the flesh" are synonymous.

I want to give you an additional text to our last study which will help you identify works of faith with "hot works." Please turn to Titus 2. Last study we discussed Titus 3:8, which tells us that those who believe should maintain good works, which are works of faith. Look at Titus 2:14. You will not notice this in the English so I need to help you a little bit here:

...Who gave himself for us to redeem us from all wickedness...

By the way, the word "wickedness" here, or "iniquity" in some translations, in the Hebrew and Greek means "to be bent towards self" when used in a spiritual sense.) So in other words, "...to redeem us from all selfishness."

...and to purify for himself a people that are his very own, eager to do what is good.

The word "eager" ("zealous," in some translations) in the Greek and the word "hot" in Revelation 3 come from the same root word. So what the text is saying is: "Through the redeeming work of Jesus Christ, He will purify a people who are on fire for good works."

You remember what description Jesus gave of John the Baptist in John 5:35? He was called "a burning light":

John was a lamp that burned and gave light, and you chose for a time to enjoy his light.

In Matthew 5:14, Jesus said to the disciples:

You are the light of the world....

"Light" and "hot" always go together.

But now I would like to continue with our study. Last week we identified works of the law as "self-righteousness," because that is what "lukewarm" is. Lukewarm works are identified with "works of the law." As I explained last study, the New Testament writers did not have a word in the Greek language which is equivalent to our English word, "legalism." So when you read that phrase, "works of the law," it's a phrase that I believe Paul coined, and he is referring to what we would call "legalism."

What is legalism? I described this as self-righteousness. Somebody asked me, "What is self-righteousness?" I will answer that question partly in this study and partly next study. But, basically, what is lukewarm? What are "works of the law"? It is the flesh, which is sinful, trying to keep the law. Does the law belong to sin or does the law belong to righteousness? In fact, Paul calls it the law of righteousness in Romans 9. So when the flesh tries to keep the law in it's own strength, that is "works of the law." Please turn to Revelation 3:16:

So, because you are lukewarm [in other words, because your works are works of the law] — *neither hot nor cold — I am about to spit you out of my mouth.*

Although oranges and grapes grow quite well in the Middle East, in the days of Christ, they had not yet learned to produce these fruits without seeds. They did not have seedless grapes or oranges. What do you do when you eat grapes and you have seeds in your mouth? You spit them out. That was a phrase that was used in the Middle East as a symbol of rejection. To "spit out" means "to reject," and we shall see this both from the Bible and the *Spirit of Prophecy.*

But here's the problem: Jesus Christ is telling us that our works are not hot, neither cold, but lukewarm. Now He makes this statement in verse 15, which we need to take note of:

I know your deeds, that you are neither cold nor hot. I wish you were either one or the other!

In other words, if we were hot, he would be happy; if we were cold, he would be able to deal with that. Because you see, both hot works and cold works are natural. What do I mean by "natural" or spontaneous?

The flesh is sinful. Therefore, the natural thing for the flesh to produce is sin! When the flesh produces sins, when you and I commit sins, we are doing something natural to our nature, which is sinful.

When the Spirit lives in us, it is natural for the Spirit to do righteousness. In fact, there's a text in the epistles of John, where it says [1 John 5:18]:

We know that anyone born of God does not continue to sin; the one who was born of God keeps him safe, and the evil one cannot harm him.

In other words, that new life, the Holy Spirit that dwells in you, does not sin. Because that Holy Spirit naturally does righteousness. So hot works are natural, cold works are natural, but lukewarm works are not natural, and I will describe this further.

But I would like to look now at what lukewarm works are not, because there are many interpretations. And then we will look at the problem and then I'll give you four reasons why God rejects lukewarm works.

We have already seen that lukewarm is a mixture of cold and hot. Now Jesus is not telling us that sometimes our works are hot and sometimes are works are cold and together that makes it lukewarm. He's not saying that. There are some who are saying that what Jesus said is that sometimes our works are hot, and other times our works are cold, and when you combine the total works, which is sometimes hot, sometimes cold, you get lukewarm. Jesus is not saying that. He's saying, "Your works are neither hot nor cold."

The only mixture is that it is the flesh trying to produce the works of the Spirit. But as far as our works are concerned, it is neither hot nor cold, but only lukewarm. So we must keep this in mind.

The second interpretation that is often used (and you may find this in some of our recent articles, there are some of our men who are saying this) is that, as a church, we used to be hot during our pioneer days. Our pioneers worked hard, they were full of sacrifice, but, as we became a bigger church, as we became more popular, we became lukewarm. So they say we were hot once, and we are moving toward cold, and at the present time we are lukewarm, and we need a revival.

One of the texts they will use is the message to Ephesus. Turn to Revelation 2:4-5. It's the first church. Here Christ is speaking to Ephesus, which is the first of the seven churches. In verse 2 he says, "I know your deeds." Then, in verse 4 and 5, He makes a statement:

Yet I hold this against you: You have forsaken your first love. Remember the height from which you have fallen! Repent and do the things you did at first. If you do not repent, I will come to you and remove your lampstand from its place.

In other words, "You were full of love but you have left it." Now that's Ephesus. But please, you can't take the statement to Ephesus and apply it to Laodicea, because Christ doesn't say to Laodicea, "You were hot once, and now you've become lukewarm." It is not right actually, to apply Ephesus to Laodicea, because the message to Laodicea does not say, "You were hot once, but you're getting warm. Watch out, or I'll spit you out."

We cannot apply Ephesus to our condition. It is true that our pioneers were hard-working. And they worked sacrificially; there's no problem there. But the works they were doing, was it works of faith or works of the law? Let me give you some evidence, maybe. that will help. I will explain why we were victims of lukewarm works during the week of prayer, when I will do the 1888 message. I'll give you the historical background that caused this problem. But right now, I'll just give you some facts.

(I'm giving you dates prior to 1888.) In 1874 from August 17 to December 19, Uriah Smith published a series of articles in the "Review," and he entitled those series: "Leading Doctrines of the Review." No mention of justification by faith. Much about the law, but no mention of justification by faith.

Three years later, in 1877, James White and Uriah Smith together held a series of studies for the ministers as part of their training. They called it "The Bible Institute." In fact, they published their lectures (that's how we know); it was a joint series for the ministers. Remember, they were training these ministers to go out and preach these messages. No mention of justification by faith. Nothing.

The following year, in 1878, Uriah Smith put out a book 336 pages long. He entitled the book, *Synopsis of Present Truth,* a summary of present truth. No mention of justification by faith or righteousness by faith, nothing.

You can see why the other Christians, because of our emphasis of the law, began to accuse us of being legalists, a stigma that we still have need to rectify today. It is for this reason that Sister White said, "We have been preaching the law and the law until we are dry as the hills of Gilboa."

But what Jesus is saying here is, "If you continue with these kinds of works, I will reject you." Now what is wrong with lukewarm works? Why is it that God and Christ will not accept lukewarm works? For example, if your child does his level best to please you, to do what is right in your eyes, are you angry or are you happy? They may not succeed completely, but they're doing their best. Wouldn't you be happy? But God is not happy with lukewarm works. First of all, are lukewarm works bad works? Are they the same as works of the flesh? No (i.e., not outwardly). What is wrong then? I'll give you four reasons:

1. When the flesh, which is 100 percent sinful, tries to be good, tries to imitate God, God's righteousness, the Bible calls that "hypocrisy." Romans 7:18 says:

I know that nothing good lives in me, that is, in my sinful nature. For I have the desire to do what is good, but I cannot carry it out.

Now when the flesh appears good, Paul calls in Galatians 6:12, "The fair showing of the flesh." Let's turn to it, Galatians 6:12. Please remember that Paul is dealing with the works of the law in Galatians; that is a problem that we are facing. The Judaizers did not make a sharp distinction between ceremonial law and moral law like we do. To them, all the laws of Moses were in one lump. The emphasis was on circumcision and the moral law.

Those who want to make a good impression outwardly are trying to compel you to be circumcised. The only reason they do this is to avoid being persecuted for the cross of Christ.

In other words, "As many as would like to show you how good you are, they'll say, 'You must to this and that.'" In their day, it was circumcision.

But I want to give you a passage, and I hope that it will show you how Jesus evaluated works of the law. Matthew 23. Please read the whole chapter yourself; I will only turn to a couple of verses here. Here is Jesus evaluating the Pharisees. Remember, the Pharisees were experts at works of the law. Please notice what Jesus is pinpointing. Matthew 23:1-2:

Then Jesus said to the crowds and to his disciples: "The teachers of the law and the Pharisees sit in Moses' seat."

Now what does Jesus mean, "They sit in Moses' seat"? They were experts in the law. Moses represents the law. To sit in Moses' seat means, "They are the authorities in interpreting Moses' law." And the Pharisees, of course, were zealous regarding Moses' law. It is to these people that He is talking. Now listen to what He is saying in Matthew 23:3:

So you must obey them and do everything they tell you. But do not do what they do, for they do not practice what they preach.

Is the problem the law? No, the problem is "works of the law"; please remember that. Then He describes the works. So that's the background. Now look at verse 5 what is wrong with the works of the Pharisees. Matthew 23:5a:

Everything they do is done for men to see.

What they're doing is good, but they want everyone else to look at them. "See how good I am!"

By the way, when you read the whole chapter, you will notice that there are two expressions that Jesus uses about these people. He calls them "hypocrites," and He calls them "blind guides." Matthew 23:27-28:

Woe to you, teachers of the law and Pharisees, you hypocrites! You are like whitewashed tombs, which look beautiful on the outside but on the inside are full of dead men's bones and everything unclean. In the same way, on the outside you appear to people as righteous but on the inside you are full of hypocrisy and wickedness [selfishness].

With this in mind, let me read you a statement that will help you. Here you will see one of the differences between lukewarm works and hot works. This is from *Steps to Christ* by Ellen G. White, page 28 and 29:

We may have flattered ourselves as did Nicodemus...

Who was Nicodemus? He was a Pharisee, a member of the Sanhedrin, so he was not an ordinary Pharisee, he was a top-class Pharisee.

We may have flattered ourselves as did Nicodemus that our life has been upright, that our moral character is correct, and think that we need not humble the heart before God....

Now please notice, she said "humble the heart," not with your words. It's easy to humble yourself with words, you know. It's easy to say, "I'm not good enough" and "I'm no good" and so on; but the heart is what Sister White is talking about.

...and think that we need not humble the heart before God like the common sinner. [In other words, "I'm better than that fellow there."] But when the light from Christ shines into our souls, we shall see how impure we are. [Now here's the statement.] We shall discern the selfishness of motive.

You know, we all face this in different ways, but sometimes when I stand out in the hall after a Sabbath sermon and somebody says to me, "Boy, that was an excellent sermon." The flesh says, "You worked hard to produce that, didn't you?" And I have to say to myself, "I don't tell that to the person because they may think I'm insulting them. Get thee behind me, Satan."

Because, you see, Satan will use the flesh to pop its ugly head up. That is why Sister White warns us about giving praise to each other. And I'll be frank with you, this is a problem I notice more in the western world than where I come from. We tend to pat ourselves on the back more here than in Africa. That's not wrong, I'm not saying it's wrong, but it is easy for us to allow the flesh to pop its head up and say, "Boy, aren't I good!"

So, please notice, she's not dealing with the act, she's saying:

We shall discern the selfishness of motive, the enmity against God....

When you go out ingathering and you work extremely hard, why are you doing it? Is it because you want to be number one in the church?" Is it works of faith or is it works of the law?

Please notice, she defines, "selfishness of motive" as:

...the enmity against God, that has defiled every act of life. Then we shall know that our own righteousness [there you have the term: our own "self-righteousness"] is indeed as filthy rags, and that the blood of Christ alone can cleanse us from the defilement of sin and renew our hearts in His own likeness.

One of the greatest works that God has to do before He lightens the earth with His glory is, if I may use that phrase from Ellen G. White, is the cleansing of the soul temple — not the outward act, but the heart, the motives.

So one difference between self-righteousness and works of faith, which is Christ's righteousness, is the motive. And you and I cannot read somebody else's motive, so we must never judge. There are only two people who can read your motives: you and God. And, to Him, it's enmity.

So the first difference is that the "works of the law" God rejects because the motive is wrong, not the act is wrong. The act is right, the motive is wrong. The Jews kept the Sabbath. They were very strict about Sabbath-keeping. They had all kinds of rules, but why were they keeping it?

I'll tell you one way to decipher if your motives are selfish. When you are very successful in God's work and you have a tendency to look down upon those who are having failure, please be warned: that is the flesh trying to tell you how good you are. By the way, even when this takes place, the devil will use the flesh to say, "Look, it was you who did it." The flesh does not want to give the Holy Spirit the credit. You know why? Because the flesh and the Spirit are enemies. Never forget that.

Okay, let's go on.

1. "Works of the law" is unbelief. Let me explain what I mean by that. In John 15:5, Jesus said:

I am the vine; you are the branches. If a man remains in me and I in him, he will bear much fruit; apart from me you can do nothing.

If you say, "No God, I *can* do something." Then you are saying, "God, you are not right." Let me give you an example. Jesus said to the disciples, "All you will forsake me." Did they agree? No. What were they guilty of? Unbelief. God said to Peter that the gospel is not only for the Jews, it is for the Gentiles. And what did Peter say? "No, they are unclean." And Jesus said to him, "What God has cleansed, don't you ever call unclean." [See Acts 10.]

Unbelief is denying God. We need to keep this in mind, because look at Revelation 3:17:

You say, "I am rich; I have acquired wealth and do not need a thing." But you do not realize that you are wretched, pitiful, poor, blind and naked.

In this verse you have two evaluations. We say that we are "rich and do not need a thing." The True Witness says that we are "miserable, wretched, and blind." Who is right? Do you believe that Jesus is telling the truth about us? Or do you think that Jesus is making a mistake? "But our works are good. Look at the reports."

Works of the law is based on unbelief. Whenever the flesh tries to do something that God says you cannot do, you are saying, "God, You are a liar." And that is unbelief. In other words, when Nicodemus was told by Christ in John 3:6:

Flesh gives birth to flesh, but the Spirit gives birth to spirit.

What did He mean? What did Jesus mean when He said, "Flesh gives birth to flesh"? He said to Nicodemus, "Let me tell you the facts: that flesh of yours can never produce righteousness. The only way you can produce righteousness is if you are born from above, or born of the Spirit."

So number two, "works of the law" is based on unbelief. We need to keep this in mind for another reason, and that is, "Is justification only by faith, or is also sanctification only by faith?"

Because this is one of the issues that we are facing. It's on the theological level, it's among our scholars, and this is what they hashed out at Palmdale some years ago.

Some of our scholars are saying that only justification is Righteousness by Faith, not sanctification. In other words, sanctification is never by faith alone, it's also my works. And, therefore, since we are sinful, we can never experience total sanctification, because I can never produce perfect works. Ford, for example, would use a statement by Ellen G. White, and she was referring to works of the law, but he applies it to sanctification. She said:

Our works are so corrupted because of the channel of the flesh, that only the righteousness of Christ can present us before God as being perfect.

And Sister White is right in terms of our standing before God. But Sister White has many statements that say it is possible through the grace of God to overcome the flesh. In fact, she makes the statement:

We need not retain one sinful propensity. [7BC 943]

That's a powerful statement. And I can give you many statements from Paul, but I want to go to number three.

3. "Works of the law" contradicts God's Agape love. In 1 Corinthians 13:5, we are told by Paul that:

[Love] is not rude, it is not self-seeking, it is not easily angered, it keeps no record of wrongs.

There is no selfishness in Agape. If I do any anything for a selfish reason, I am contradicting Agape. In other words, if there is a selfish motive, that is not Agape. I'll give you an example. In Matthew 19:27, Peter comes to Jesus and He says:

"We have left everything to follow you! What then will there be for us?"

"What is our reward?" Now was that works of the law, or works of faith? Why did Peter forsake all? Was it to please Christ or because he believed that Christ was the Messiah? He believed that the Messiah would overthrow the Romans and he wanted to be one of the top cabinet ministers. How do I know? Because when Jesus came to wash the feet of Peter, Peter said, "You will never [he used a very strong Greek word] wash my feet." Here's the scene from John 13:6-9:

He came to Simon Peter, who said to him, "Lord, are you going to wash my feet?"

Jesus replied, "You do not realize now what I am doing, but later you will understand."

"No," said Peter, "you shall never wash my feet."

Jesus answered, "Unless I wash you, you have no part with me."

"Then, Lord," Simon Peter replied, "not just my feet but my hands and my head as well!"

Now Jesus knew his heart, so Jesus simply said this, "If I don't wash your feet, you will have no part in my kingdom." In other words, "Forget your Prime Minister's position."

"Oh, "he says, "in that case, wash not only my feet but my head and my hands and everything, because I want to be number one."

Jesus knew how to deal with the flesh. So please remember that, while works of the law may appear good outside, they are devoid of Agape and, therefore, to God are filthy rags.

4. The fourth reason why works of the law are wrong — and this is an important one — is that works of the law deny Christ as our Righteousness. That's a denial of Christ's righteousness. Let me give you a text, Galatians 5:4-5, especially verse 4:

You who are trying to be justified by law have been alienated from Christ; you have fallen away from grace. But by faith we eagerly await through the Spirit the righteousness for which we hope.

Now what was the Galatian problem? Were the Galatians having the same problem as the Jews? The answer is no. The Jews wanted salvation entirely by their own works. The Galatians fell for another trap: it was legalism, but a subtle form of legalism. The Galatians fell for the idea that it is not enough to accept Christ as your righteousness, you must also contribute by being circumcised and keeping the law. In other words, "I am saved by faith plus works."

Let me read you a quotation from *Faith and Works* by Ellen White. Please read that first whole chapter, because Sister White is dealing with the problem. Reading from page 20:

Should faith plus works...

That's Galatianism. And, by the way, this was the problem after 1888. Before 1888, we were strong legalists. After 1888, we got into deeper waters because of the Galatianism problem. But let me give you the quotation:

Should faith plus works purchase the gift of salvation for anyone then the Creator is under obligation to the creature. Here is an opportunity for falsehood to be accepted as truth.

And then she goes on to say that this is exactly where the Roman Catholics have gone wrong. Because the Roman Catholic church teaches that you are saved by faith plus penance; you have to do penance when you confess your sins.

When I went to confession, I could not come out of that confessional box free, I had to do penance. And, you know, we young kids, teenagers, we were smart. We would watch and see which priest was in which box, because some of them gave you long penance, and some of them gave you short penance, depending on their disposition. One of them enjoyed giving us long penance, and none of the kids went to him. We would wait. So there was a big line here, waiting for that kind-hearted priest, and a short line for the other priest. These were the old folks, who wanted to do penance, who felt that the more penance you did, the more God would accept you, these went to him. We kids went to the other fellow; all we wanted was absolution from our sins. So we were doing works, we were confessing our sins, plus penance. Sister White says that if we add works to faith, we are no different than a Roman Catholic. In other words, folks, if you are guilty of lukewarm works:

1. You are a hypocrite,

2. You are guilty of unbelief,
3. Your works are devoid of agape, and
4. You are denying Christ as your righteousness.

Both, I would like to add, both imputed and imparted righteousness must be all of Christ. What the world needs to see is not me, but Christ dwelling in me and living in me. So when Jesus says [Matthew 5:14a]:

You are the light of the world.

...the word "light" is in the singular in the Greek, "you" is in the plural. We are many, but there's only one light, folks, and that light is Jesus Christ. The world needs to see Christ. It is only when Christ lives in us through the Spirit that we will do the works of Christ, out of pure Agape love.

I would like to read some more quotations before ending:

To those who are indifferent at this time [that is the 1888 message] Christ warns us, "Because thou art lukewarm and neither cold nor hot, I will spue thee out of my mouth." The figure of spewing out of His mouth means that He cannot offer up your prayers or your expressions of love to God, He cannot endorse your teaching of His word or your spiritual works in any wise, He cannot present your religious exercises with the request that grace be given you. [6T 408]

Why? Because the motive is selfish, folks. One more quotation from *Review and Herald,* 15 December 1904:

Satan is seeking with all his ability to corrupt mind and heart. [Please notice what he's trying to corrupt — mind and heart.] And how successful he is in leading men and women to depart from the simplicity of the gospel of Christ. Ministers and church members are in danger of allowing self to take the throne.

Folks, we are always in that danger:

Ministers and church members are in danger of allowing self to take the throne.

And it is because of self, folks, that there was opposition to that precious message in 1888. It was self that was at the heart of the problem. And it was there because our works are lukewarm. With this in mind, we will now be able to look at verse 17, because lukewarm works are very deceiving. We will see how it has deceived us and that will be our next study on verse 17.

CHAPTER FIVE

LAODICEA IS DECEIVED

Revelation 3:17:

You say, "I am rich; I have acquired wealth and do not need a thing."
But you do not realize that you are wretched, pitiful, poor, blind, and
naked.

We have discovered so far, spending the last two studies on
verses 15 and 16, the true significance of our lukewarm condition,
which we saw is the works of the law, or self-righteousness, or
legalism. And once we have discovered this, we have actually laid
the foundation for a true and for a meaningful study of the
Laodicean message.

This study, I would like us to consider verse 17. In verse 17,
the "True Witness," which is Christ, shows us how our lukewarm
works, or our "lukewarmness," our works of the law or legalism,
has deceived us. When you look at the verse, you will find that
we can divide this verse into two parts: the first half of this verse
is Laodicea's own self-opinion of her spiritual condition, and the
second half is Christ's evaluation, or reaction, to our own opinion.

As you see the text, you will discover that the two opinions
totally disagree. There's a contradiction here, of what we think of
ourselves, and what Christ's evaluation of us is. Besides this, you
will discover that there is a subconscious problem; for Jesus says:

But you do not realize....

Let's look at the verse first of all:

You say [i.e., the angel of Laodicea, with her followers, is saying], *"I am rich; I have acquired wealth and do not need a thing* [that is our self opinion]." *But you do not realize* [this is Christ now evaluating our opinion] *that you are wretched, pitiful, poor, blind, and naked.*

So you can see clearly that there is a contradiction on what we say about ourselves, or what we think about ourselves, and what Christ says about us. Now, number one, why is there a disagreement? Number two, what did Jesus mean when He said, "But you do not realize"? Well, He means that we have been deceived, we have been honestly deceived. And the reason we have been deceived is because we have not clearly distinguished works of the law [which are lukewarm] from works of faith, which are hot.

And so I would like to start off, to show you, that there is a subtle difference between works of the law and works of faith. And it is very easy to be confused. In fact, Martin Luther and the Reformers were confused over this so that they condemned anyone who presented works of faith. And Luther defined James' epistle (at the end of his life he admitted James was inspired) but he said that James was not an inspired book. He called it a "straw epistle," which in German meant it carried no weight. Paul was the correct, inspired man.

Actually, we will discover that Paul and James totally agree. What Paul condemns is not works of faith, what Paul condemned is works of the law. He does uphold, with James, works of faith. Paul believes that genuine justification by faith actually produces works.

Let me start by giving you some texts to show you that Paul condemns works of the law but upholds works of faith. Please turn to Romans, we'll start with Romans. Romans 3:20:

Therefore no one will be declared righteous in his sight by observing the law; rather, through the law we become conscious of sin.

Please notice, Paul is condemning anyone who is trying to go to heaven by the works of the law, no one will make it. Then in verse 28 of the same chapter:

For we maintain that a man is justified by faith apart from observing the law.

In other words, Paul is saying that works of the law contradicts justification by faith, it's an enemy. He will bring this out in Galatians, even here he will bring it out in Romans that you cannot have both. So Paul looks at works of the law, as I mentioned before, as what we would call legalism, self-righteousness.

Turn to Galatians 2:16, you will find the same thing. And when you look at this in its context, you will discover that he is making this statement to Peter, who had sidetracked from the gospel when he separated from the Gentiles and began to eat with only the Jews. And Paul is simply quoting to the Galatians what he told Peter:

...Know that a man is not justified by observing the law, but by faith in Jesus Christ. So we, too, have put our faith in Christ Jesus that we may be justified by faith in Christ and not by observing the law...

So please remember to Paul, works of the law is a contradiction to justification by faith. So he ends the verse:

...because by observing the law no one will be justified.

This was part of his public rebuke to Peter.

Turn to one more text, Galatians 5:4, where Paul says that anyone who tries to add works of the law to justification by faith, this is not simply justification by faith against works of the law, this is people trying to add works of the law to justification by faith. He says:

You who are trying to be justified by law have been alienated from Christ; you have fallen away from grace.

You can't mix the two.

But, in contrast, I would like to show you that Paul upholds works of faith, so that he is in harmony with James, who is trying to defend justification by faith which produces works, i.e., works of faith. In Ephesians 2:10, Paul says that while works do not contribute towards our salvation one bit (that's verse 9) in verse 10 he says:

For we are God's workmanship, created in Christ Jesus to do good works, which God prepared in advance for us [we who believe] *to do.*

So Paul is in harmony with James. Turn to 1 Thessalonians, see what he says to the Thessalonians, for what they were doing to help the Jewish church in Jerusalem with their blessings, with their offerings and their good works. 1 Thessalonians 1:2-3 (verse two gives the introduction). He says:

We always thank God for all of you, mentioning you in our prayers. We continually remember before our God and Father your work produced by faith, your labor prompted by love [please notice: works of faith are always a labor of love], *and your endurance inspired by hope in our Lord Jesus Christ.*

One more text, Titus 3, there you will find Paul saying two things. In verse 5 he says:

...He saved us, not because of righteous things we had done, but because of his mercy. He saved us through the washing of rebirth and renewal by the Holy Spirit,...

So please notice, our works do not contribute towards our salvation at all. But in verse 8 it says:

This is a trustworthy saying. And I want you to stress these things, so that those who have trusted in God may be careful to devote themselves to doing what is good. These things are excellent and profitable for everyone.

Not to you, but to "everyone." In other words, it is a revelation to all that you are a witness to Christ. In fact, I gave you a text last time, I'll repeat it, Titus 2:14, talking about Jesus Christ:

Jesus Christ, who gave himself for us to redeem us from all wickedness and to purify for himself a people that are his very own, eager to do what is good.

That word "eager" ("zealous" in some translations) in the Greek is the same root word as "hot" in Revelation 3.

So there is a complete harmony. Okay, with this in mind I would like to make a statement, because there is some confusion. You remember that people will say that Abraham obeyed or kept the statutes. All the Old Testament men who were commended for their good works, were commended because of their works of faith.

I'll give you an example. Please turn to Hebrews 11. You can say the same thing about Noah but here's a good example. Hebrews 11. This is the chapter on faith. Look at verse 8:

By faith Abraham, when called to go to a place he would later receive as his inheritance, obeyed and went, even though he did not know where he was going.

Please notice, he did not know where he was going, but he obeyed the call of God. It was an obedience of faith. He didn't ask God, like some missionaries will ask the General Conference, "Is there electricity where I'm going, are there fridges, is there...?" If you say, "No," then they say, "Okay, I'm not going."

God did not tell him, there is a house there waiting for you, there is running water. God said, "I want you to go to a land which I will give you." That was faith.

Let's look at Noah. God said to Noah, "I'm going to destroy this world with a flood. I want you to build an ark." Did Noah believe? Yes, what was the evidence of his belief? Works. You see, works of faith are based on the promise of God. Works of the law are based on your promise. God said, "Here is My law." And the Jews said, "All that you say we will do."

But now the question must come: What really is the difference between works of the law and works of faith? Because remember, it's works of the law that have deceived us. What's the difference? We need to see it, because works of the law and works of faith are very much similar in the outward acts. The difference is not so much in the works themselves, both look similar outwardly.

In other words, you can have two people keeping the Sabbath, one is doing works of faith, and one is doing works of the law. What is the difference? You can have two people going out ingathering, one is works of the law, one is works of faith. They look similar outwardly, so that it is very easy to confuse one for the other. So what's the difference?

There are two major differences. The first difference is the origin, the source. One is man's efforts, by the flesh. The other one is Christ doing it through faith. Let me give you an example. I want you to turn your Bibles to Luke 18. Here is an excellent example of works of the law. And I want you to notice the number of times the word "I" appears. The works are good, but notice the origin. Who is doing it? Luke 18:10-12. This is Jesus speaking. I want you to notice the introduction to the parable, this is crucial. Jesus is discussing here works of the law. Verse 9 is the introduction:

To some who were confident of their own righteousness and looked down on everybody else, Jesus told this parable:

Now here is one difference. Normally, a person who does works of the law always despises others. They look down upon others. Continuing with verse 10:

"Two men went up to the temple to pray, one a Pharisee and the other a tax collector.

Now who is a Pharisee? What did the word "Pharisee" mean to the Jew? (Not to us Adventists, because we have given the word "Pharisee" a negative meaning.) But to the Jew, "Pharisee" did not have a negative meaning. A Pharisee was looked upon as a very holy person. You know why? Because a Pharisee was zealous about the law. We would call them "Holy Joes" today. They were the "holy people"; they were the "gurus" of Paul's day. Listen to the Pharisee in verse 11:

The Pharisee stood up and prayed about himself...

Now by the way, the standing up was common. It was quite common for the Jews to stand up praying. The idea of kneeling was only in times of crises, but the normal attitude for praying was standing up. The fact that this Pharisee prayed standing was only custom. Listen to what he prayed. He prayed thus with whom? With Himself. He's telling God something. He's not asking God; he's telling God about himself.

The Pharisee stood up and prayed about himself: 'God, I thank you that I am not like other men — robbers, evildoers, adulterers — or even like this tax collector. I fast twice a week...'

Is it wrong to fast twice a week? Is it a sin? No. Is it good? Yes, it's good; nothing wrong with that.

'...and give a tenth of all I get.'

Isn't that good? Boy, he would get a star in his crown if he was here. So please notice, the works are not bad, they're good: "I fast twice a week, I give tithes of all that I possess." Was he doing works of faith, or was he doing works of the law? Works of the law.

What was wrong with his works? Number one, it made him feel good about himself. So who was he living for? For God, or for himself? Himself. He's telling God, "God, please look at me, see how good I am."

Do you know what Christ will say to him in the judgment? Look at Matthew 7:22:

Many will say to me on that day, 'Lord, Lord, did we not prophesy in your name, and in your name drive out demons and perform many miracles?'

"I have preached in your name, I have cast out devils in your name, I have done many wonderful works in your name. Surely I should have a place in heaven."

And what does Jesus say? Verse 23:

Then I will tell them plainly, "I never knew you. Away from me, you evildoers!"

Please remember, the Hebrew word "iniquity" (in some translations, which here is "evildoers") to the Jew meant "living toward self," because the word "iniquity" means "bent towards self."

So the works of the law are always done for our glory, for ourselves. The source is the flesh. Can the flesh actually do good works? No. It cannot do genuine good works. Can it perform good works? Yes. So please remember that the source is wrong.

By the way, you notice the use of the word "I" as the Pharisee prayed, talking about himself? "I fast twice in the week, I give tithes of all that I possess." What does tithe paying really represent? It is a confession that all that I possess doesn't belong to me, but to God. But "This is mine, look God, I'm helping your church, your church cannot do without me, so I surely deserve some credit."

Okay, now turn in contrast to two other texts, Philippians 3. I want to show you how Paul throws away works of the law, which he was famous for as a Pharisee, in exchange for Christ. I want you to notice the attitude of works of faith. Philippians 3:3, what does it say there, it says that "Our confidence is in Christ Jesus and not us." Here is the text:

For it is we who are the circumcision, we who worship by the Spirit of God [not in the letter, but in the Spirit, from the heart], *who glory in Christ Jesus, and who put no confidence in the flesh....*

Philippians 3:9:

[I want to] be found in him, not having a righteousness of my own that comes from the law [i.e., the works of the law], *but that which is through faith in Christ — the righteousness that comes from God and is by faith.*

Verse 10:

I want to know Christ and the power of his resurrection and the fellowship of sharing in his sufferings, becoming like him in his death,....

In other words, "I want Christ to live in me now that I've accepted Him as my Righteousness."

But now I want you to turn to 1 Corinthians 15 where Paul does deal with works of faith, but he doesn't use that expression, but as you see it you will discover what he's talking about. In verse 9 Paul says:

For I am the least of the apostles and do not even deserve to be called an apostle, because I persecuted the church of God.

Verse 10:

But by the grace of God I am what I am, and his grace to me was not without effect. No, I worked harder than all of them — yet not I, but the grace of God that was with me.

Have you got it? Paul is saying, "I worked more than all of them." Of course, "them" refers to the Apostles. "I have worked more than the Apostles. But," he says. There's a "but" there. But what?

Yet not I, but the grace of God that was with me.

"It was not I who was doing the work, it was God doing it in me. I was just an instrument." So one difference is the origin.

The second difference is the motivation. And I've already touched on this a little bit. Works of the law is always motivated by self. In other words, we do works of the law for three reasons:

1. Fear of punishment.
2. Because I want a reward, I want to go to heaven.
3. Because of glory for me.

Works of the law is always motivated by self. Either fear of punishment, like the man in Matthew 7:22 says, "Lord, I have done all these things; I deserve heaven." So it's a desire for reward or for self-glory.

Let me give you a couple of texts, one from the New Testament, one from the Old. Matthew 23. By the way, read the whole chapter. There Jesus condemns works of the law as hypocrisy, which is correct, because the flesh when it pretends to be good is hypocrisy. Hypocrisy means "pretending to be something you are not." And we are sinners by nature; how can you pretend to be something good? That's hypocrisy. Okay, Matthew 23:5:

Everything they do...

This is talking about the Scribes and the Pharisees. Remember, the works they do are good works. Am I being clear? In other words, "All the good works they do..."

Everything they do is done for men to see...

That's why they prayed in public. They made a big show. It says here:

They make their phylacteries wide and the tassels on their garments long....

"Our dress is going right up to the ankle!" There's nothing wrong with this. The motivation was to see how holy they were. Turn to verses 26-28 of Matthew 23. It says:

Blind Pharisee! First clean the inside of the cup and dish, and then the outside also will be clean.

You see, they were cleaning only the outside but the inside was dirty. He's talking about their condition. Verses 27-28:

Woe to you, teachers of the law and Pharisees, you hypocrites! You are like whitewashed tombs, which look beautiful on the outside but on the inside are full of dead men's bones and everything unclean. In the same way, on the outside you appear to people as righteous but on the inside you are full of hypocrisy and wickedness.

You know, folks, our problem is that we judge ourselves by our acts. God judges us by our motives. That is why in Matthew 5 Jesus brings this out. The Pharisee would say, "I have never committed murder."

Christ says, "One moment. If you hate somebody in your heart, even though you don't kill him in the act, if you hate him in the heart without a reason, you have committed murder. If you look at a woman to lust, even if you haven't done the act, you have committed adultery."

Folks, God looks at the heart! That is why in the judgment, God will judge every secret motive. Okay, now I want to give you a text from the Old Testament, Proverbs 16:2. When you realize this you will know that all of us are like unclean things. Proverbs 16:2:

All a man's ways seem innocent to him, but motives are weighed by the Lord.

Not the acts, but the spirit behind the acts. And this is something that we need to know.

Turn to Galatians 4 where Paul gives us an example of works of the law, and works of faith (which is the fruit of the Spirit) in the context of the two covenants. Remember, the Old Covenant is man promising to be good so that he may have a right to heaven. In the New Covenant, man is accepting by faith the promises of God and allowing Him to do the works. That's the difference between the two covenants. Galatians 4, let's start with verse 21:

Tell me, you who want to be under the law, are you not aware of what the law says? For it is written that Abraham had two sons, one by the slave woman and the other by the free woman. His son by the slave woman was born in the ordinary way...

What did Paul mean by that statement? He's simply saying that the son born of the slave woman — that is Hagar — was the product of Abraham's works.

...but his son by the free woman was born as the result of a promise.

Who produced Ishmael? Abraham. Who produced Isaac? God. Could Abraham produce Isaac at the time he was born? Why not? Because Sarah had passed the age of child bearing. It was impossible, and that is why God waited to show Him that works of faith are works produced by God in those who have faith. And he goes on in verse 24:

These things may be taken figuratively, for the women represent two covenants. One covenant is from Mount Sinai and bears children who are to be slaves: This is Hagar.

Why Mount Sinai? Because when God gave the law at Mount Sinai, what did the Jews say? "All that You say we will do." That was the old covenant, man promising God to be good. Did they succeed? No. And when they failed, did they acknowledge it? No, instead they made rules, human rules that they could keep, and they said, "God, we are keeping your law." And Paul goes on to say in verse 25:

Now Hagar stands for Mount Sinai in Arabia and corresponds to the present city of Jerusalem, because she is in slavery with her children.

And so Paul will make the statement in Galatians 5:1:

It is for freedom that Christ has set us free. Stand firm, then, and do not let yourselves be burdened again by a yoke of slavery [legalism].

Galatians 4:26:

But the Jerusalem that is above is free [i.e., without any of our works], *and she is our mother.*

And, by the way, what does the Bible say? Verse 28:

Now you, brothers, like Isaac, are children of promise.

But there is something that you need to know about; it's painful. Verse 30:

But what does the Scripture say? "Get rid of the slave woman and her son,...

Now please look at the application: "Get rid of the slave woman and her son..,." Who does the slave woman and her son represent? Works of the flesh.

...for the slave woman's son will never share in the inheritance with the free woman's son.

Now was Abraham trying to please God when he produced Ishmael? Yes. Was he trying to rebel against God, or was he trying to fulfil God's promise? So please remember, Hagar with her son represents works of the law produced by the flesh. Isaac represents God's promise and God's performance through Sarah.

Okay, I want to conclude, and there's two things I want to do now. First of all, I want to read some statements. This is from *Steps to Christ*, by Ellen G. White, pages 44-45:

"There are those who profess to serve God while they rely upon their own efforts to obey His law, to form a right character and secure salvation."

Please notice, they do it, and their motive is to secure salvation.

"Their hearts are not moved by any deep sense of the love of Christ, but they seek to perform the duties of the Christian life as which God requires of them in order to gain heaven."

Please notice, this is works of the law.

"Such religion is worth nothing."

Okay, the next statement is something that we need to remind ourselves of constantly:

"The birth of a son to Zecharias, like the birth of the child of Abraham, and that of Mary, was to teach a great spiritual truth, a truth that we are slow to learn and ready to forget."

So even after we learn it, we forget it. What is this truth? Here it is:

"In ourselves, we are incapable of doing any good thing."

That's both before conversion and after conversion: "In ourselves." (When we deal with Romans 7, it comes out very clear there.)

"But that which we cannot do will be wrought by the power of God in every submissive and believing soul. It was through faith that the child of promise was given; it is through faith that spiritual life is begotten and we are able to do the works of righteousness." [DA 98]

Please notice, it is only through faith that we can produce righteousness. In other words, both justification and sanctification are by works of faith. It is by faith alone.

Okay, here are some statements, just simple sentences (all by Mrs. White):

"All our good works are dependent on a power outside of ourselves." [COL 159]

Have you got it? "All of our good works are dependent on a power outside of ourselves." Not "part of our good works" but "all of our good works."

"Of ourselves we can do nothing good." [1SM 101]

And one more:

"All that man can do without Christ is polluted with selfishness and sin. But that which is wrought through faith is acceptable to God." [1SM 364]

Now, why am I emphasizing this? Because of this, folks. I don't know how many of you remember, but the first major issue on Righteousness by Faith in our church, that is in modern times, in the 20th century, that we tried to solve.... You see, we were very heavy on legalism; then we sent our scholars to worldly universities, and they came back with an Evangelical gospel of Righteousness by Faith, and it produced a controversy in our church, in the 1960s. And then they tried to solve the problem when they met at Palmdale.

Do you remember Palmdale, where they met some years ago, where the scholars and the administrators met to solve the issue of Righteousness by Faith? One of the biggest issues in that conference was to define Righteousness by Faith. What is the definition? The administrators said, "It is both justification and sanctification." If you read the first article in the *Review and Herald* for the week of prayer by Neil Wilson, that's how he presented it, as both justification and sanctification.

The scholars said, "No, only justification is by faith; sanctification is never by faith alone. We have to do something." And this controversy has not yet ended. But please remember, the moment you add "I" to sanctification, you are still in the Laodicean condition. Whether you talk of our standing before God in terms of justification, or whether you talk about sanctification, Christ living in you, it is "not I, but Christ."

Now it's true, faith is always a struggle, because what does faith mean? It means two things, not one but two. Faith means:

1. Not I,
2. But Christ.

The "not I" is the most difficult part, because when we say "not I," we are saying something that is contradicting our nature; we are going against our nature when we say, "not I." So that's painful, and we want some credit in sanctification so we say, "I plus Christ. Only justification is by faith alone." But that is not true, the Bible doesn't teach it. The Bible teaches that the flesh is enmity with God, it is not subject to the law of God, and can never be. Folks, it has to be, "not I but Christ" in everything. And that is what Christ is saying.

But our works, which look good, works of the law, have deceived us, because it resembles works of faith. And we think we are "rich and do not need a thing," but what does Christ say?

You are wretched, pitiful, poor, blind, and naked.

In concluding this verse, I would like to say this, that the word, "wretched," Christ's evaluation of us, appears twice in the New Testament, twice! Only twice in the Greek in the whole of the New Testament. The first time, it is found in Romans 7:24, where Paul says:

What a wretched man I am! Who will rescue me from this body of death?

The second time is in the Laodicean message where Christ says that we do not know that we are "wretched." I believe that only when we can say, "What a wretched person I am," then we can say with Paul (verse 25):

Thanks be to God — through Jesus Christ our Lord!

"I can do all things through Jesus Christ," but we can only do that when we say, "What a wretched person I am." And the only way we can say, "What a wretched person I am" when we realize that our works of the law, good as they may seem, are in God's eyes filthy rags and sin. So may God bless us that we may understand this.

73

CHAPTER SIX

LAODICEA IS COUNSELED

Revelation 3:18:

I counsel you to buy from me gold refined in the fire, so you can become rich; and white clothes to wear, so you can cover your shameful nakedness; and salve to put on your eyes, so you can see.

We saw in our last study that we have been deceived, so that while we think "we are rich and have acquired wealth and have need of nothing," the True Witness shatters our false security by telling us that we do not know — and that's the big problem, we "do not realize" that we are really "wretched, pitiful, poor, blind, and naked." Terrible.

But thank God, folks, the True Witness does not stop there. Thank God that our situation is not hopeless. As we turn to Revelation 3:18, which is what we will cover in this study, we will discover that the True Witness would like to give us hope for our situation. So there is a hope. In fact, Christ offers a complete remedy for our three-fold problem. Let's look at verse 18 and then I will show you what the remedy is in connection with verse 17. Having told us our problem in verse 17, that we are wretched, miserable, poor, blind, and naked, Jesus goes on and says in verse 18:

I counsel you to buy from me gold refined in the fire, so you can become rich; and white clothes to wear, so you can cover your shameful nakedness; and salve to put on your eyes, so you can see.

I counsel you, I advise you to buy of me:

1. Gold refined in the fire, so you can become rich;
2. White clothes to wear, so you can cover your shameful nakedness; and
3. Salve to put on your eyes, so you can see.

In other words, for our poverty and wretchedness, Christ offers us gold tried by fire that we may be rich. For our miserable nakedness, He offers us white raiment that we might be clothed, that our nakedness not appear in the judgment especially. Then, for our blindness, He offers us eye salve. So there are three remedies for our three-fold condition. But I want you to look at one word here, it is very important. This precious, heavenly merchandise is not free. You have to *buy* them. Please notice verse 18:

I counsel you to buy....

There is a price that has to be paid. Now normally, when you look at these things, what they signify — the gold tried in the fire, and the white clothes, and the eye salve — when you look at these things in Scripture, you will discover that they are free gifts of God. Then why does God say to Laodicea, "You must buy"? Well, folks, they are free gifts only to those who are "poor in spirit." But to people who are self-righteous like the Jews were, it is not free. Let me give you a text and show you how God addressed Israel. Turn your Bibles to Isaiah 55. This was the prophet that God was using to try to bring the people out of their Laodicean condition. You see the Jews had a problem that was similar to ours. Their problem was self-righteousness. Isaiah 55:1. This is the typical cry of a salesman in a market place:

Come, all you who are thirsty, come to the waters; and you who have no money, come, buy and eat! Come, buy wine and milk without money and without cost.

Now, it doesn't make sense, it seems to be a contradiction, you buy, but without money. So if it's without money, the question is:

"What is the price?"

First of all, we need to understand the word, "buy" as it is used here. In fact, it's the same meaning as we use it in our everyday terminology. The word "buy" means to exchange something that you have for something that you want. That's the basic meaning. In the days of the Bible, they would often exchange goods. If I had too much corn growing in my garden, I would take it to the market and exchange it for wheat. That is "buying."

Let us say you're in the mall and pass a shoe shop and you see a lovely pair of shoes and it is $150. And you say, "Boy, that's expensive, but I like it." And you stand there and you say, "Should I get it?" You see, you have $150, which is yours, which you earned through hard work, but the question is, "Should I give this up for a pair of shoes?" That is buying. The word, "buying" is "exchanging."

Now Laodicea does have something that is very, very valuable to her. It is the basis of our pride, even our denominational pride is based on that, and that is our righteousness. I want to give you an illustration: I was holding a lay-workers seminar there in Ethiopia. And it was a long seminar, it was three weeks. These were lay-farmers — most of the lay people there are farmers, peasant farmers — and certain times of the year, like I suppose in winter here, they do not have much work to do. So they have free time and we used to pull them in and give them some good Bible studies, and this was a three-week course. At the end of the second week, I got a telephone call from the Union Headquarters telling me that there was a leader of the church from the General Conference, from the Sabbath School Department, "Could you please step down and let him have the lay people for three days since they're already there?"

So I thought, "Sure, no problem." And he was trying to explain to them how to increase the Sabbath School offering. Now in Ethiopia they collect offerings with a bag connected to a stick, and they put it out because people sit very close together, it's crowded. And he said, "That's the worse thing to do, because you can put your hand in and pretend you are giving, and give nothing. Or you can put your hand in and take out money and nobody will know. What you need is an open plate. And it must have no felt on it, an open plate that makes a noise, so people can hear whether you're giving copper or silver. And the deacons who collect the money must be the first ones to give, and they must show the people what they're giving to set a good example. I guarantee you, the Sabbath School offering will increase."

One of our dear sisters, a student at the University of Haile Selasie — it was closed down because of the Marxist Revolution — she stood up and said, "Elder, with all due respect to you, what you are teaching us sounds very much like the flesh. If we have the love of Christ, we will give." The other lay-people said, "Amen."

Of course, that made him annoyed, and he said to them, "Are you trying to tell me that you know the gospel and I don't?"

She said, "No, but it doesn't sound right to us."

Well, he went and reported this problem to the president of the college, and the president of the college said, "Well, maybe what you are teaching is contradicting what Pastor Sequeira is teaching, so you need to see him!"

The president came and told me about it, even some of the lay people came and told me what had happened. You see, I wasn't there, I had just stepped out and was letting him teach them. Well, I'll tell you, he didn't come to me and so the last day, the third day, I said to my wife, "Let's invite him for supper, maybe in our home we can open up the subject."

So we did invite him and he didn't open up the subject, so I did. I wanted to clarify the issue. He wanted to rebuke me, but he did not do it directly so he did it through another man. He was telling me how terrible this man was, and, of course, the man was Morris Venden. He said, "This man has all the young people in his hands, but what does he do with these incentives? He makes mockery out of them."

I turned around to him and said, "Maybe Morris Venden is right."

Then he made a statement to me, which reflects very much on what we are studying, he said to me, "Are you saying to me that I have to give up 45 years of successful ministry for the

Righteousness of Christ?"

I said, "That is what it may cost you."

Folks, it is not easy when you have had tremendous success in the Christian life to give it up for the Righteousness of Christ; it's very expensive. I want to give you an example. Please turn to Philippians 3. You see, the thing is this, the more success you have, the harder it is. And I want to turn to a man who was very successful, because what God is saying to Laodicea, "You must give up your self-righteousness which you think has made you rich, you must give it up, in exchange for My Righteousness."

Before we look at Philippians 3, let me read a couple of statements from the pen of Ellen G. White to give you a background:

"The people of God are represented in the message to the Laodiceans as in a position of carnal (which is another word for fleshly) security. They are at ease, believing themselves to be in an exalted condition of spiritual attainment." [3T 252]

"I asked the meaning of the shaking I had seen (The angel of the Lord showed Ellen G. White in vision that there would be a shaking in this church) and was shown that it would be caused by the straight testimony called forth by the counsel of the True Witness to the Laodiceans...."

What is the counsel? "To buy from Me" these three things.

"...This will have its effect on the heart of the receiver and will lead him to exalt the standard and pour forth the straight truth. Some will not bear this straight testimony, they will rise up against it and this will cause a shaking among God's people." [1T 181]

It happened in 1888, it will happen today, folks. Then the next statement, which is related to this same issue, *Testimonies to Ministers,* pages 64-65 (remember, they're the angels of Laodicea):

"They (referring to ministers) are not willing to be deprived of the garment of their own self-righteousness. ("We worked hard for this; why should we give it up?") They are not willing to exchange (which is another word for "buying") their own righteousness, which is unrighteousness, for the righteousness of Christ, which is pure unadulterated truth.

Which is "not I, but Christ" — no mixture of self in it.

So please remember this is the issue. Now I want to turn to this example, and that is Philippians 3. If there was anyone in the Jewish church, which was famous for self-righteousness, who had a claim to a wonderful success, it was Paul before his conversion. And in verse 4, 5, and 6 He puts in a nutshell what he had attained, number one by birth, number two as a Pharisee, and by performance. Verse 6:

...As for zeal, persecuting the church...

"Regarding zeal for God (that's what he means), I persecuted the church."

In other words, "I was on fire for you, God, and when I persecuted the church, I was not doing it in rebellion towards You, in my mind I was serving You."

As for legalistic righteousness, [I was] faultless. But whatever was to my profit I now consider loss for the sake of Christ.

He was willing to give up all his success for Christ's righteousness. And that is "buying." He goes on to say in verse 8:

What is more, I consider everything a loss compared to the surpassing greatness of knowing Christ Jesus my Lord, for whose sake I have lost all things...

Please notice, it does involve suffering, it does hurt our pride, individually, and denominationally. But it says clearly (verses 8-9):

I consider them rubbish [dung or refuse], *that I may gain Christ and be found in him, not having a righteousness of my own that comes from the law* [i.e., the works of the law], *but that which is through faith in Christ — the righteousness that comes from God and is by faith.*

Please notice there are two "righteousnesses" in verse 9: (1) his righteousness, which he had attained by much effort and tremendous success, and (2) God's righteousness, which is yours by faith alone. He had to give up one for the other. This, folks, is the price. It is a costly price. As our brother said in Ethiopia, "Do you want me to give up 45 years of successful ministry?"

Yes folks, God wants you to give up everything. He wants us to give up our opinion about ourselves, He wants us to give up all that we thought was profit, because it was not, and we must turn to Christ as our Righteousness, both in terms of justification and also sanctification. We must be clear: the 1888 message did not preach only justification as the Righteousness of Christ. Both. The formula for Justification, the formula for Sanctification is the same: "Not I, but Christ." That is the expensive price. So I've spent some time on the word "buy" because that's the key word in Revelation 3:18.

Are you willing to give up your self-opinion, and all the success that has given you ("stars in your crown")? Are you willing to give it up for the Righteousness of Christ? That is the price we have to pay.

This folks, is what will produce the shaking, and there will be some who will not be willing to give up, especially those who have had success. And I'll tell you about the people who have had success: normally they're people with very strong wills. You see, people with strong wills have a tremendous success. I don't know how many of you have attended a Five-Day Non-Smoking program. You will notice that people with strong wills have more success than those who have weak wills. Very often it is these strong-willed people who give you a hard time in committee meetings. And they give you a very hard time in discipline committees. They come down hard upon people. They say, "Look, I had no problem with this. I was a heavy smoker and I gave it up; it was nothing. Why are these people having such a problem?"

Well, folks, all our success is filthy rags. In other words, what we think is very valuable to us, which is self-righteousness, please remember, in God's eyes it is filthy rags. And if you want a text, look at Isaiah 64:6. Isaiah was talking to a people who had a similar problem. Let me read it to you:

All of us have become like one who is unclean, and all our righteous acts are like filthy rags; we all shrivel up like a leaf, and like the wind our sins sweep us away.

Please notice that by nature we are unclean and, because of that, "all our righteous acts are like filthy rags."

So remember, in God's eyes our righteousness is as filthy rags. Now I want to turn back to Revelation 3:18 and examine those three items, the three items of merchandise from heaven that are offered to Laodicea if she is only willing to buy or to exchange.

The first is gold tried by fire.

What is this gold tried by fire? What is it? I want you to turn to 1 Peter and let's get a clue. 1 Peter 1:7, because here we have a clue from the Bible. Let's read verse 6 also to get the whole impact:

In this you greatly rejoice, though now for a little while you may have had to suffer grief in all kinds of trials.

Are you being discouraged by "all kinds of trials"? Peter is trying to give you some comfort. Verse 7:

These have come so that your faith — of greater worth than gold, which perishes even though refined by fire — may be proved genuine and may result in praise, glory and honor when Jesus Christ is revealed.

The words, "gold refined by fire," in the Hebrew thinking, in the Old Testament, is simply "purified faith," faith that has been purified. And in the New Testament, that faith that has been purified is known as "the faith of Jesus Christ," because the faith of Jesus was purified.

You remember in Gethsemane, if you read Mark 14:32 onwards, three times Jesus prayed to His Father, "Father, please remove the cup, nevertheless not My will but Thine." He did not allow self to have any part in His ministry. And every dross of self was crucified in the life of Christ. Now when we first accept Christ our faith is egocentric. In other words, we accept Christ because we're either afraid of punishment or because we want to go to heaven. That's the normal basis of accepting Christ. But what Christ wants to do is to purify this faith from its egocentric motivation. He wants us to have what Paul says in Galatians 5:6. He wants us to have "faith which is motivated by love." And that's the process, that's the growth that He wants us to have.

I would like to read at this time three or four statements by Ellen G. White which are dealing with this:

"Faith and love are golden treasures, elements that are greatly wanting among God's people...."

Don't we have faith? Yes, we have faith, but it is ego-centric faith. We must give this up for the faith that is of Christ, the faith that is motivated by love, the selfish faith for Christ's faith.

"...Unbelief is closing their eyes so that they are ignorant of their true condition. The True Witness does describe their blindness." [3T 255]

"The gold tried in the fire is faith which works by love. (Which is a quotation from Galatians 5:6.) Only this can bring us into harmony with God. We may be active, we may do much work, but without love, such love as dwelt in the heart of Christ, we can never be numbered with the family of heaven." [COL 158]

In other words, we can never reflect the character of Christ. So there has to be a growth here. Now please remember, we must be careful when we read this that we don't read in the context of Justification. She's talking here in terms of the evidence of Justification which must be reflected more and more, the life of Christ.

"The gold here recommended as being tried in the fire is faith and love. It makes the heart rich for it has been purged until it is pure and the more it is tested the more brilliant is its lustre."

Please notice, it is faith that "has been purged." Purged of what? Of self.

"Love to God is the very foundation of religion. To engage in His service merely from hope of reward or fear of punishment (which is the basis of self-righteousness) would avail nothing."

These are statements that clearly point out that "gold tried in the fire" is "faith which worketh by love." So that is what Christ is offering us. He says, "I want to offer you My faith, which is motivated by love, rather than your faith which is egocentric."

The second item that He's offering us is white clothes (or "raiment" in some translations). What is white raiment? The

Righteousness of Christ. Imputed or imparted? Both! Let me give you a couple of texts; let me first of all give you the imputed Righteousness of Christ, i.e., it is imputed righteousness which qualifies us for heaven. Please remember that. It is not imputed Righteousness plus imparted Righteousness that qualifies for heaven. Imputed Righteousness is what qualifies us for heaven. Turn to Romans 9, and please remember that imputed Righteousness is something that is done outside of us, what was accomplished in the holy history of Christ. Romans 9:30 up to the end. And I want you to look at something here that is very much linked with the Laodicean message. Remember what He says in Revelation 3:18?

I counsel you to buy from me ... white clothes to wear, so you can cover your shameful nakedness....

Please keep that in mind as we look at Romans 9:30:

What then shall we say? That the Gentiles, who did not pursue righteousness, have obtained it, a righteousness that is by faith...

So here's the Gentiles which sought righteousness by faith. Verse 31:

...but Israel, who pursued a law of righteousness, has not attained it.

So here are two groups of people. The Gentiles accepted Christ as their Righteousness; the Jews tried it by keeping the law. Two different methods, old and new covenants. Who succeeded and who failed? The Gentiles succeeded and the Jews failed. Why did they fail? Verse 32:

Why not? Because they pursued it not by faith but as if it were by works. They stumbled over the "stumbling stone."

And that is something that we must keep in mind. What Paul is saying here is that there can be no mixture of Christ our Righteousness and self-righteousness. It's either one or the other. You can't blend the two together. The moment you accept Christ's Righteousness, you must give up self-righteousness. The moment you uphold self-righteousness, Christ's Righteousness becomes a stumbling block, an offense to you. Now look at verse 33:

As it is written: "See, I lay in Zion [which is another term for Israel] *a stone that causes men to stumble and a rock that makes them fall..."*

It is a rock of offense to whom? To the poor in spirit or to the self-righteous? The self-righteous.

"...and the one who trusts in him will never be put to shame."

Please notice, if you "buy the white clothes" you "will not be ashamed" because "you will be clothed." And you may remember that I read you a statement from the *Spirit of Prophecy* (by Ellen G. White) that "self-righteousness is not the wedding garment." If you try to go to heaven by your righteousness you will appear what? Naked. Why? Because in the judgment, God doesn't look only at the act, He will look at the motive. And self-righteousness is always motivated by self. That's why it's called self-righteousness. So please remember that the white raiment is the Righteousness of Christ imputed. It is also the Righteousness of Christ imparted. Now turn to Revelation 19:7-8. These verses are in the context of the last days, it's dealing with the same people, the last generation of Christians:

Let us rejoice and be glad and give him glory! For the wedding of the Lamb has come, and his bride has made herself ready.

Christ has been waiting for years to reproduce His character in His bride, that she may be ready. How did she make herself ready? Verse 8:

Fine linen, bright and clean [there's the white raiment], *was given her to wear." (Fine linen stands for the righteous acts of the saints.)*

Is it something they have produced, or is it something that they are experiencing? Is it something that they have produced? No! It is the righteousness of saints because it is the righteousness of Christ imparted to the saints. Please notice:

Fine linen, bright and clean, was given her to wear....

Who clothes her? Christ. By the way, it's this text that led the western world to have a white garment for a wedding dress for the bride. It symbolized purity. They are changing these days, and they have good reason to do that.

I want to read a statement here from *Testimonies*, Volume 4, by Ellen G. White. Just notice how she puts it in terms of 1888:

"Fearful is the power of self-deception on the human mind. What blindness, setting light for darkness, and darkness for light. The True Witness counsels us to buy of Him gold tried in the fire, white raiment, and eye salve. The gold here recommended as having been tried in the fire is faith and love, it makes the heart rich for it has been purged until it is pure. And the more it is tested the more brilliant is its lustre. The white raiment is purity of character, the Righteousness of Christ imparted to the sinner...."

That's how she defines the white clothes in this Laodicean message.

"...This indeed is a garment of heavenly texture (you did not produce it, it's of heavenly texture) that can be bought only of Christ for a life of willing obedience...."

And if you look at the context, what she means is not willing obedience in the sense of our obedience. "Willing obedience" means I am willing to say, "Not I," that's my obedience, so that I may receive the Righteousness of Christ. The price I pay is "Not I." In exchange Christ gives me His righteousness. Then she goes on to that third item:

"The eye salve is that wisdom and grace that enables us to discern between evil and good and to detect sin under any guise." [4T 88]

Do you know self-righteousness is sin? But it doesn't appear as sin. It looks good. But this eye salve makes us see it without any guise. Now please, going back to the scripture itself. Christ is offering us white raiment that we may be clothed. What is the context of the Laodicean message? "I know your deeds." So please notice, the context is, "I know your deeds." Is it hot? Is it cold? Is it lukewarm? He wants our works to be hot. How can our works be hot? The imparted Righteousness of Christ. So the context is works, that's the key phrase of the passage. So God is offering us not only imputed righteousness that we may be clothed in the judgement and not appear naked, but that we may also be clothed in our experience, that Christ may be able to be reflected through us.

Now I want to review another statement. It's dealing with the chapter "The Time of Trouble" in *The Great Controversy*, page 621. Do you know why God allows the last generation of Christians to go through the time of trouble? It's part of the work of producing the righteous character of Christ. It is part of the "buying" of that white raiment. Listen to this: talking about the time of trouble:

"Their affliction is great. The flames of the furnace seem about to consume them, but the Refiner will bring them forth as gold tried in the fire...."

Please notice, the time of trouble is part of that counsel that He's offering us. What will we have to give up in the time of trouble? Any ounce of holding on to self-righteousness.

"....God's love for His children during that period of their severest trial is as strong and tender as in the days of their sunniest prosperity..."

So does God's love diminish in the time of trouble? No.

"...but it is needful (i.e., the time of trouble is needful for them) to be placed in the furnace of fire that their earthliness must be consumed, and the image of Christ may be perfectly reflected."

Not for our salvation, but that the world may see, that the gospel is the power of God unto salvation. And God will say, "Here are My people, who have the faith of Jesus. You can try them, you can try them to the very limit, you can't kill them, but you can try them."

And as we are tried, folks, what will come out is faith which is motivated by love. Our anchor will not be our love for God, but God's love for us. Our faith will be in His love, not in His judgment. We will look at God not as a Judge Who's ready to punish you, but a God Who loves us even though we are going through the furnace.

What held Jesus on the cross? Why did He not come down and save Himself? Could He not do that? He could, but He believed that His Father had not forsaken Him. He felt forsaken as far as His feelings went. But His faith was in the love of God which never fails. And that is why I have said before and I will repeat again if there is any passage that you need to memorize it is Romans 8:35-39:

Who shall separate us from the love of Christ? Shall trouble or hardship or persecution or famine or nakedness or danger or sword? As it is written: "For your sake we face death all day long; we are considered as sheep to be slaughtered." No, in all these things we are more than conquerors through him who loved us. For I am convinced that neither death nor life, neither angels nor demons, neither the present nor the future, nor any powers, neither height nor depth, nor anything else in all creation, will be able to separate us from the love of God that is in Christ Jesus our Lord.

Who will separate us from the love of God?

Is your faith in the love of God and His righteousness which He gave us in Jesus Christ?

And, of course, finally, I don't have to go into any more detail, it is the eye salve. In the Middle East they used a black ointment. You see, in the olden days they did not have sunglasses and the sun is very powerful in the Middle East. And they used this black stuff which kept the eyes cool and helped you to face the glare of the sun, so that you could see. Otherwise you had to squint your eyes and you couldn't see properly and so the eye salve was used here as a symbol of the Holy Spirit opening our eyes. Please notice, it is the Holy Spirit that must guide you into all truth. John 16:13-14:

But when he, the Spirit of truth, comes, he will guide you into all truth. He will not speak on his own; he will speak only what he hears, and he will tell you what is yet to come. He will bring glory to me by taking from what is mine and making it known to you.

The Holy Spirit is the only One Who can open our eyes and show us that our righteousness is filthy rags.

When Christ comes to you as individuals and says, "Look, will you please buy? Will you please give up your own self-opinion? Will you give up all your success and all those badges that the church gave you for the tremendous work you have done? Are you willing to call that dung in exchange for the righteousness of Christ?" how will you answer?

You have to make a choice. I know what choice I am going to make, because I have discovered that the only righteousness that will qualify me for heaven is not my successful ministry, it is not the number of people I baptized in Africa, it is Christ and His Righteousness. That is the only thing that will qualify me for heaven. And it is my prayer that this is the only Righteousness that you will accept.

In preparation for our next study please look at verse 19, because there is a problem. It seems that Laodicea doesn't want to buy the gold easily. So He has to do something else to us to put sense into our head:

Those whom I love I rebuke and discipline. So be earnest, and repent.

So it seems that it is not going to be easy for us to buy, so God in His patience has to do something else besides offer us His wonderful, rich merchandise from heaven. May God help this church that we may reflect the character of Christ because we have bought the gold tried in the fire, the white clothes, and the eye salve.

CHAPTER SEVEN

LAODICEA IS REBUKED

Please turn your Bibles to Revelation 3, I want you to look at a passage that is important to us. It would be wonderful if the Laodicean message would have ended with the counsel of verse 18, but, unfortunately, it doesn't. And it seems that, like the Jews, we have been kind of stiff-necked and stubborn. And the result is this, that God had to take a further step. He doesn't stop at verse 18. And this further step is verse 19 which is what I would like to look at today: God rebukes and chastises Laodicea. Verse 19:

Those whom I love I rebuke and discipline. So be earnest, and repent.

Before we actually look at this passage I would like to read some *Spirit of Prophecy* (by Ellen G. White) quotes found in 1T 181 and 185:

"The testimony of the True Witness has not been half heeded. The solemn testimony upon which the destiny of the church hangs has been lightly esteemed, if not entirely disregarded. This testimony must work deep repentance and all that truly receive it will obey it and be purified."

That's a clear statement. The next one:

"The message to Laodicea has not accomplished that zealous repentance among God's people which I expected to see. And my perplexity of mind has been great."

Here's the cry of the messenger of the Lord. And you know folks, I am convinced that the reason why the second coming has been delayed is not because of an unfinished work, but because of an independent work. We are trying to do it, maybe subconsciously, of ourselves. And I am convinced that bigger budgets, and better quality printing and paper, and more sophisticated gadgets will never finish the work, important as they may be.

When I first came to Walla Wall, Washington, in 1982, just three or four weeks after I arrived, there was a big evangelistic effort held in the Treasure Valley, and all of us Pastors had to take part in it. It was a new experience for me. The evangelist had 13 projectors and three screens and a computer. I was just amazed, coming from the [African] bush, to see this computer working, and these projectors. I said to myself, "Boy, if we had this in Africa maybe we would baptize them by the thousands."

But we baptized only 26 in that effort: 10 of them were children from our schools who were already on their way to baptism, and another five were people who had already been ready for baptism before the evangelistic effort. And I said, "With all that money we spend, and all those gadgets, the result was very poor."

I believe there has to be a work done. I don't know if you are familiar with the statement by Ellen G. White concerning the message of "Justification by Faith" that came to this church in 1888. She said the work of this message is to take "the glory of man and put it in the dust." Unless that takes place, unless we can say from the heart, "Not I," Christ cannot take over completely and fulfil his work and cut it short in righteousness.

Okay, having laid this foundation, let's look at verse 19, let's analyze it. The first thing I want you to notice is how He begins, the rebuke and the chastening:

Those whom I love...

So I thank God that He doesn't rebuke us, and He doesn't chastise us out of anger. He does it out of deep concern for his people.

Those whom I love I rebuke and discipline.

Turn to Hebrews chapter 12, because God did the same thing to the Jews. I want to remind you of verse 6-12. Please notice what he says there. Verse 6:

...Because the Lord disciplines those he loves, and he punishes everyone he accepts as a son.

And then he goes on to explain. He first compares it to a human chastening and then he explains why. Verses 7-8:

Endure hardship as discipline; God is treating you as sons. For what son is not disciplined by his father? If you are not disciplined (and everyone undergoes discipline), then you are illegitimate children and not true sons.

And then he goes on to explain in verse 9 that our human fathers sometimes chastened us not out of love but out of anger; they wanted to give vent to their feelings. Look at verses 9-10:

Moreover, we have all had human fathers who disciplined us and we respected them for it. How much more should we submit to the Father of our spirits and live! Our fathers disciplined us for a little while as they thought best; but God disciplines us for our good, that we may share in his holiness.

Then he goes on to explain in verse 11:

No discipline seems pleasant at the time, but painful. Later on, however, it produces a harvest of righteousness and peace for those who have been trained by it.

Please notice, it has to be exercised, we have to be trained. And so verse 12 says:

Therefore, strengthen your feeble arms and weak knees.

Stop being discouraged, God has a purpose.

Well, let's go back to Revelation 3:19:

Those whom I love I rebuke and discipline....

Do you know that God loves us? He loves us in spite of our failures. He loves us because his love is unconditional. Because He loves us He does two things: Those whom I love...

1. I rebuke and
2. I discipline.

Now the word, "rebuke" means "to scold" or "to tell off," "to correct," "to reprove," and normally the word, "rebuke," as used in this text, has to do with verbal rebuke. In other words, God scolds us or rebukes us because we have not listened to the counsel.

For example, you remember Jesus was telling the disciples that he was going to die, and you remember Peter grabbed hold of him and he said, "This can never happen to you." It's found in Mark 8. You remember what Jesus said to him? Mark 8:33:

But when Jesus turned and looked at his disciples, he rebuked Peter. "Get behind me, Satan!" he said. "You do not have in mind the things of God, but the things of men."

That was a rebuke. He was rebuking Satan for using Peter as a tool. "Get behind me, Satan!"

If you go to Mark 16:14, you will notice that Christ is rebuking the eleven disciples, one of them was not there, he was rebuking them for their unbelief. And the word in the King James is, "He upbraided them." He rebuked them for their unbelief concerning His resurrection.

Or if you look at John 12:7, you will see that Jesus is rebuking those who were criticizing Mary:

"Leave her alone," Jesus replied. "It was intended that she should save this perfume for the day of my burial."

"Leave her alone," He says. So a rebuke normally refers to a verbal correction. And God has sent this church, just as He sent to the Jews, many times, rebukes, especially through the Messenger of the Lord. In fact I want you to look at this statement. The reason I want you to look at it is because it was penned in 1891, if I remember correctly, a time when we thought we were progressing. Listen to what Ellen G. White says. It's found in 5T 719, 720:

"The rebuke of God is upon us because of our neglect of solemn responsibilities. His blessings have been withdrawn because the testimonies He has given have not been heeded by those who profess to believe them."

Please notice, He rebukes us, and we don't accept it. And in 1888, they were not even listening to her.

"O for a religious awakening. The angels of God are going from church to church, doing their duty, and Christ is knocking at the door of your hearts for entrance, but the means that God has devised to waken the church to a sense of their spiritual destitution have not been regarded. The voice of the True Witness has been heard in reproof (and that's the rebuke) but has not been obeyed. Men have chosen to follow their own way instead of God's way because [please notice] self was not crucified in them thus the light [i.e., the truth as it is Christ] has had but little effect upon minds and hearts."

This is a tragedy, folks. So God is rebuking, and He's rebuking, and He says, "Look, won't you please listen to Me." But you know, after rebuking, and you don't listen, God has to take a greater step, a much tougher step. And that is the next word: "Those whom I love, the first thing I will do is, I'll rebuke you. And if you don't listen, I will discipline you."

Now the word "discipline" ("chasten" in some translations) means "to punish," not in the sense of eternal punishment, because that would give none of us any hope, but to punish in terms of correcting. And the punishment could be physical, it could be economical, it could be political. But it is normally something that happens to you that is allowed of God for a purpose.

Now I want to give you an example: the Babylonian captivity. For years, God tried his level best to get the Jews to turn from idolatry, but they would not listen. He corrected them, He rebuked them from prophet after prophet, and, finally, as a last resort, He said, "I'm going to chastise you. I'm going to allow a foreign, pagan government to take you into captivity." And so we have the Babylonian captivity.

Why did God allow the Babylonian captivity? It was his final resort. And folks, if we don't listen to God, He's going to do the same thing to us. I don't know what it will be, it could be a financial collapse, it could be something, and we would be desperate, our whole system would come into trouble. The Babylonian captivity was devastating to the Jews.

In the study of Hebrews, I gave you a series of texts which talks about this, "Whom God loves He chastises." I called it the "refining work of God. Read them for yourself when you get a chance, because it has important lessons. These are the texts that talk about the refining process of God. And remember, the main purpose is what Hebrews 12 brings out, "Whom God loves He will chasten."

Now some of it is because of our stubbornness, some of it is because of refining us. Remember the experience that Jesus illustrated in John 15, "I am the vine and you are the branches. And if I want to produce fruit in you I have to prune you." Pruning is always painful, but it has a beautiful purpose. Deuteronomy 8:5:

Know then in your heart that as a man disciplines his son, so the Lord your God disciplines you.

Job 5:17:

Blessed is the man whom God corrects; so do not despise the discipline of the Almighty.

Psalm 94:11-15:

The Lord knows the thoughts of man; he knows that they are futile. Blessed is the man you discipline, O Lord, the man you teach from your law; you grant him relief from days of trouble, till a pit is dug for the wicked. For the Lord will not reject his people; he will never forsake his inheritance. Judgment will again be founded on righteousness, and all the upright in heart will follow it.

Now these are all texts that deal with this same subject. Proverbs 3:11-12:

My son, do not despise the Lord's discipline and do not resent his rebuke, because the Lord disciplines those he loves, as a father the son he delights in.

Isaiah 48:10-11:

See, I have refined you, though not as silver; I have tested you in the furnace of affliction. For my own sake, for my own sake, I do this. How can I let myself be defamed? I will not yield my glory to another.

Malachi 3:1-3:

"See, I will send my messenger, who will prepare the way before me. Then suddenly the Lord you are seeking will come to his temple; the messenger of the covenant, whom you desire, will come," says the Lord Almighty. But who can endure the day of his coming? Who can stand when he appears? For he will be like a refiner's fire or a launderer's soap. He will sit as a refiner and purifier of silver; he will purify the Levites and refine them like gold and silver. Then the Lord will have men who will bring offerings in righteousness,

And then, in the New Testament, John 15:2:

He cuts off every branch in me that bears no fruit, while every branch that does bear fruit he prunes so that it will be even more fruitful.

That's the one I just mentioned about the vine and the branches. Romans 5:3, 5:

Not only so, but we also rejoice in our sufferings, because we know that suffering produces perseverance; ... And hope does not disappoint us, because God has poured out his love into our hearts by the Holy Spirit, whom he has given us.

Part of the refining process to reproduce God's love in us, 2 Corinthians 4:15-18:

All this is for your benefit, so that the grace that is reaching more and more people may cause thanksgiving to overflow to the glory of God. Therefore we do not lose heart. Though outwardly we are wasting away, yet inwardly we are being renewed day by day. For our light and momentary troubles are achieving for us an eternal glory that far outweighs them all. So we fix our eyes not on what is seen, but on what is unseen. For what is seen is temporary, but what is unseen is eternal.

Then, of course, Hebrews 12:5-14:

And you have forgotten that word of encouragement that addresses you as sons: "My son, do not make light of the Lord's discipline, and do not lose heart when he rebukes you, because the Lord disciplines those he loves, and he punishes everyone he accepts as a son." Endure hardship as discipline; God is treating you as sons. For what son is not disciplined by his father? If you are not disciplined (and everyone undergoes discipline), then you are illegitimate children and not true sons. Moreover, we have all had human fathers who disciplined us and we respected them for it. How much more should we submit to the Father of our spirits and live! Our fathers disciplined us for a little while as they thought best; but God disciplines us for our good, that we may share in his holiness. No discipline seems pleasant at the time, but painful. Later on, however, it produces a harvest of righteousness and peace for those who have been trained by it. Therefore, strengthen your feeble arms and weak knees. "Make level paths for your feet," so that the lame may not be disabled, but rather healed. Make every effort to live in peace with all men and to be holy; without holiness no one will see the Lord.

And a couple from Peter: 1 Peter 1:3-7:

Praise be to the God and Father of our Lord Jesus Christ! In his great mercy he has given us new birth into a living hope through the resurrection of Jesus Christ from the dead, and into an inheritance that can never perish, spoil or fade — kept in heaven for you, who through faith are shielded by God's power until the coming of the salvation that is ready to be revealed in the last time. In this you greatly rejoice, though now for a little while you may have had to suffer grief in all kinds of trials. These have come so that your faith — of greater worth than gold, which perishes even though refined by fire — may be proved genuine and may result in praise, glory and honor when Jesus Christ is revealed.

1 Peter 4:12-14:

Dear friends, do not be surprised at the painful trial you are suffering, as though something strange were happening to you. But rejoice that you participate in the sufferings of Christ, so that you may be overjoyed when his glory is revealed. If you are insulted because of the name of Christ, you are blessed, for the Spirit of glory and of God rests on you.

Now all these texts deal with this one purpose, and that is to refine us.

But now, in the Laodicean concept, going back to Revelation 3, why does God rebuke us, why does He discipline us, what for? Why does He take these drastic measures? Well, look at verse 19:

Those whom I love I rebuke and discipline. So be earnest, and repent.

Both of them — "rebuke" and "discipline" — are in the present tense. He will continue doing this until we become "zealous" and do what? Repent.

Now it's very interesting, the word "earnest" (or "zealous" in some translations), the word that John uses here, the Greek word is *zaylowoe*, is the same root word as the word, "hot," *zestos* in this Laodicean message. You remember, Jesus, the True Witness says, "You are neither hot nor cold." And we discovered that "hot" refers to works of faith which originate with God and are motivated by love; whereas "lukewarm" works are works of the law which outwardly appear good but in God's eyes are filthy rags. And what God is saying is, "I want you to turn hot in terms of your works by repenting. Be zealous, therefore, be fervent, and repent."

Now the word "repent" simply means "a change of mind." That's what the word means, *meta noia*, two words, change of mind. A good way of explaining it is a U-turn. You're driving on the freeway, and you discover that you forgot something like your airline ticket — I'm talking from experience — and you make a U-turn so that you may get it.

Works of the law is living a life independent from God. So what God is saying here is that "I want you to make a U-turn." In what sense are we to repent? Now we must look at the context. We need to remind ourselves of verse 17. What does verse 17 say? It is an evaluation of us. The evaluation is two-fold. We have our own opinion of ourselves and we think, because works of the law have deceived us, that we are "rich and increased in goods and have need of nothing." Christ says, "You do not know that you are wretched, miserable, poor, blind, and naked."

Now there are two opinions here of ourselves. One is ours, one is Christ's. To repent means to give up our opinion of ourselves and accept Christ's. And if we don't do that, we will have to learn it the hard way. I'll give you an example: one of the disciples of Christ, well, the others too, but especially one who had to learn the hard way through chastisement, and that is Peter. Turn to Luke 22. This is an incident that took place at the Passover feast where Christ instituted the Lord's supper. Luke 22 and we will look at verse 31 onwards. Jesus turns to Peter after the Lord's supper in verse 31, and the Lord said:

"Simon, Simon,..."

Whenever the Jews repeated a name twice or repeated a word twice, it was for emphasis. "Pay attention, Peter," He is saying.

"Simon, Simon, Satan has asked to sift you as wheat."

In other words, Satan would like to pull you out of Christ. You see, in the Middle East they sifted wheat on a basket. They threw the wheat up and the wind would blow away the chaff. And Satan would like to treat you like chaff to get rid of you out of Christ.

"But I have prayed for you, Simon, that your faith may not fail."

Please notice. What was Satan trying to destroy? Satan was trying to destroy Peter's faith, and that's always his plan. When he discourages you, when he makes life difficult for you, he has one objective, to destroy your faith. And so Jesus is telling Peter:

"But I have prayed for you, Simon, that your faith may not fail. And when you have turned back [i.e., when your faith becomes unshakeable and when you have really understood the truth], strengthen your brothers."

Now I want you to notice Peter's response, verse 33:

But he replied, "Lord, I am ready to go with you to prison and to death."

In other words, "What on earth are you talking about? My faith fail you? You are mistaken, Lord. You may be right about the other fellows. I am ready to die for you. How can you talk about my faith failing you, and praying for my faith. I don't need your prayers. I am Peter." He didn't say, "I am the first Pope" but he could have said almost that. "I am infallible, I can never fail you."

Well, did he fail or not? Yes, he did. And that is why, folks, Jesus put Peter through a very bitter experience, an embarrassing experience in John 21. This is after the resurrection when Peter had failed and he was broken and he repented. I want to remind you that, even though Peter failed, Jesus did not say to him, "I told you so, now you suffer." He did not do that. Do you know the first thing that Jesus did even before He met Peter, even before he appeared to any one of the disciples? He told Mary through the angel — remember, Mary was in the tomb and the angel spoke — He told Mary through the angel, "Please tell the disciples *and Peter.*"

You see, in the Jewish system, in the Jewish mentality, if you denied your God ("Yahweh," to the Jews), if you denied Him with cursing and swearing, and this is what Peter did the third time, you had committed the unpardonable sin, there was no hope for you. God could not forgive you, that was the Jewish teaching. So when Peter denied his Lord with cursing and swearing, being a Jew with his Jewish mentality he felt that there was no hope for him. And Jesus said, "Yes, there is hope for you. I knew all along that you would deny me. I told you, but you wouldn't listen to me. But I want you to know, Peter, that I have not forsaken you. Even though you did not believe me and you failed, I want you to know that you are still my disciple."

That's why the angel singled out Peter, because if Mary had told the disciples, "The angel told me that I will appear to the disciples," Peter would have said, "That doesn't mean me." But Jesus wanted Peter to know that he was part of the disciples even though he had failed.

Now we need to know this because there are many today that say the Adventist church no longer belongs to Christ, it's Babylon because it has failed. Folks, God is very longsuffering, He's very patient. He has been rebuking us, and to some degree He has chastised us. We have had some crises, but nothing to what He will put us through if we don't listen.

Peter had to learn the hard way, and in John 21 after the resurrection, Jesus met the disciples by the Sea of Galilee, and in verse 15, after they had breakfast, you remember Jesus asked him twice, "Do you *agape* Me?" and Peter replied, "I *phileo* You." And it's important that you understand the play of words, which is not in the English language. Jesus was asking the question, "Do you love Me unconditionally?" That's the question, because the word, "agape" means "unconditional love." And Peter replied, "I love You," but used *phileo*, a human love which is fluctuating and unreliable. And Peter said, "Lord, You know that I *phileo* You."

In other words, "You knew Lord, you knew all along, but now I admit that you are right." Peter had repented, folks. He had admitted, "You are right, I was wrong." He repeats it the second time, and, of course, the third time Jesus kind of switches and says, "Is this the only kind of love you have for Me?"

Because the third question in verse 17, "Simon, Son of Jonas," Jesus did not use the word *agape,* He used the word, *phileo.* "Phileoest thou Me?" In other words, "Peter, is this the only kind of love you have for Me, this human love, which is unreliable, which fails?"

And Peter was grieved, it was embarrassing. But he admitted, he was a converted man now. He said, "You know all things. (You know what's inside me, even more than I did.) You know that I *phileo* You." (That's all I'm capable of.)

And Jesus was not discouraged, He said, "Now I can use you."

In all the three statements Jesus said, "Feed My lambs." "Feed My sheep." and "Feed My sheep." Why? Because God cannot use us, folks, fully, unless we have lost confidence in ourselves.

There is a statement, I could not find the reference but you can look for it, where Sister White says:

"When God's people put self aside and make room for the Holy Spirit to take over, the work will be finished."

And that is what God is looking for. We need to repent, folks, repent, number one from our pride, whether it's individual pride or denominational pride, we must repent. We must say, "Lord, we have failed You." Just like Paul said, "You claim to know the truth. You claim to understand what is right and what is wrong from the law of God, but you have blasphemed the name of God in the eyes of the world."

One day, one of the members of our church came to my house and brought me a document. It's a document that was requested, it was a survey that was requested by our denomination by a firm that takes polls of different issues. And this investigation was to see what was the situation of the American people in North America regarding religion, regarding church going, regarding the Adventist church, and regarding their view of Adventist literature.

They took three cities: Pittsburgh [Pennsylvania], Des Moines [Iowa], and Seattle [Washington]. Pittsburgh was primarily dominated by Roman Catholics. Therefore, they hardly listened to us; they knew very little about us. Des Moines was a mixture of Catholics and Protestants. Of the three cities Seattle was the worst. They said the majority of the inhabitants of Seattle are non-church goers, are not interested in religion. The ones that are interested are mainly Protestants. So there are very few Catholics, they said.

Number one, in all three cities, but especially Des Moines and Seattle, the people who were not going to church said, "We do not need religion, because there is in man a certain amount of goodness. What we need is a better interchange of human relationship." So they were doing the mistake of what Romans was condemning.

Number two, the people who were in Seattle, said that they found the literature that was put out by Adventists — mainly regarding Revelation Seminar pamphlets — was revolting. "It presented a God Who is out to punish you, the emphasis is fear...." That's what they said. And they said, "Some of the pictures on these pamphlets look almost like pornography." Very few of the non-Adventist people found it appealing. So it was quite devastating to find out what people thought about us. It was quite negative, in all three areas, mainly Seattle.

So while we, God's people are boasting, people have a very low opinion of us, according to this investigation. And I think that they're going to send this to all the Pastors. This came through a private source. By the way, the survey was made in Seattle on October 18, 1988. So it's not too old.

You know, you only have to mix with other Christians and you will discover that most of them have a very low opinion of us, as Christians. They don't think of us as a loving people, they think of us as a proud, self-righteous people. When I was chaplain of Nairobi University, there were five chaplains; I was the only Adventist. Of the others one was a Baptist, one was a Lutheran, one was a Roman Catholic, and there were two interdenominationals: World Vision was one of them and the other represented Campus Crusade.

And when I began mixing with them, one day the Baptist Minister said to me, "You know, you're the first Chaplain of the Adventist Church who is willing to mix with us. All the others gave us the impression that we were dirt."

And this is the impression that some of us have given. You know: "You are Philistines, we have nothing to do with you." You need to read one of the Calvinistic scholars, who has written a book about us, it's about Adventism. He is from Grand Rapids [Michigan]. He wrote it as a text book. And one of the big issues he deals with is the word, "Remnant." He says, "Adventists admit that there are true Christians in all denominations, but they are the only ones who are the Remnant."

Now you see, the word "Remnant" means, "the faithful ones." So he goes on to say, "In other words, they think that we are third-grade Christians, because they are the only ones who are faithful to God." And so this is the kind of thing that is coming across from the other people.

But the thing is, folks, that is not the big issue. The big issue is, are we willing to say, "God, You are right." Are we willing to say, "God, we have failed to reveal to the world Your character of love." Have we failed? Because you see, the negative talk about us is not always the main issue, because they talked negatively about Christ Himself, they talked negatively about the early Christian church.

But the big issue is, Christ is saying to us, "I want you to repent. I want you to give up your opinion about yourself, and I want you to take your righteousness and put it in the dust, and accept My white clothes, accept My faith, accept My eye salve. Open your eyes and see." And that is the cry of God.

And so I would like, in closing, to look at this quotation, because it is a statement that we need to look at:

"The Lord calls for a renewal of the straight testimony borne in years past..."

Now, remember, we dealt with this in our last study. The "straight testimony" is the counsel to Laodicea. The counsel is God's remedy for our lukewarmness. For us to accept that counsel, there has to be repentance, zealous repentance.

"...He calls for renewal of spiritual life. The spiritual energies of His people have long been torpid [which is another word for lukewarm]. But there is to be a resurrection from apparent death. By prayer and confession of sin we must clear the King's highway. As we do this the power of the Spirit will come to us. We need the Pentecostal energy. This will come, for the Lord has promised to send His Spirit as the all-conquering power." [GW 307-8]

Please notice, there is no sign here of, "You are Babylon!" There is a plea for us to repent, there is a plea for us to turn round. And I want to remind you of the disciples. The disciples at the Passover feast, where Christ instituted the Lord's Supper, they were full of confidence in themselves. Every one, not only Peter, but every one disagreed with Christ when He said, "All of you will forsake Me." They were full of confidence; therefore, they were full of self; therefore, they were always fighting. And even at the Lord's supper, they were fighting which of them would be the greatest. This is also found in Luke 22.

But after the cross, that was the means of shaking the disciples. You see, the ambition of the disciples was egocentric, they were looking for Christ to establish His kingdom on this earth and each of them was thinking, "I will be the Prime Minister," and "I will be the Finance Minister," and so on. And I suppose you have the same thing every time we have an election. We join parties and those who are close friends of the candidate say, "Boy, when you get into power, I hope you will give me a high position." And I suppose everyone is anxiously waiting to see who he will choose to be his cabinet ministers.

The disciples had that same mentality. Then the cross took place. And you know what happened? Their hopes were dashed to pieces. You remember the two men returning home to Emmaus, and Jesus met them, do you remember what they said to Jesus? "We thought He was the One. We thought He was the One Who would have restored the Kingdom and established....but now He's dead. Our hopes are dashed." They were downcast. Their hands were down, their knees were feeble, and Jesus had to open their eyes.

These same disciples, 40 days later in the upper room, were of one heart and one mind. Self was crucified; they experienced a deep repentance. They had turned from self to Jesus Christ; the cross had done its work in their lives. And folks, we have to experience the same thing. Self must be crucified. It is painful, and God demands it. It is the only way because the formula of the gospel is "Not I, but Christ." And when that takes place in this church, and in this denomination, when we in repentance say, "God, I admit that in me there is nothing good. All the sins that have been done in this world I am capable of. When I see what Hitler did, and what Idi Amin did, and I realize that these men have the same nature as I do, that given the chance, and the environment, and the circumstances, I am capable of doing what these men did."

We look at the holocaust and say, "Boy, I don't know how those Germans could do it." The reason they did it is because they turned their backs to God. When Hitler turned his back to God, then you have unrighteousness. And folks, when this country turns its back to God, we in America are capable of doing exactly what Hitler did. And we are doing it to some extent, when we agree to have abortion.

And so, my dear people, it is important that we repent. I hope that God doesn't have to chastise us anymore. We must realize that God loves us, He has a concern for us. Let us surrender to His testimony. Let us admit that we do not know that we are wretched, miserable, poor, blind, and naked, that He is right, and that our only hope is to accept the heavenly merchandise, so that we may be filled with His Spirit and His power, and we will turn the world upside down. That is my prayer.

CHAPTER EIGHT

LAODICEA MUST REPENT

Revelation 3:19:

Those whom I love I rebuke and discipline. So be earnest, and repent.

I want to remind you that repentance means "a change of mind" or "a change of direction." If we were to describe it in modern terms, "repentance is a U-turn." It's changing direction, it can be both physically or of the mind.

Now in what sense does God want us to repent? We must always be clear and look at the context, because repentance in the Bible is always specific. For example, when Peter preached at Pentecost, and the people said, "What shall we do?" after he told them that they had crucified the Son of God and he said, "Repent." It was repentance in terms of the crucifixion.

Repentance in the Bible is always specific. We need to ask ourselves, "In what sense is Christ asking us to repent?" And the answer is in two senses. They are related, we need to have a change of mind in regards to verse 17, because in verse 17 we say that we are rich and increased with goods, and Christ says that we are "wretched, miserable, poor, blind, and naked." Now we need to have a change of mind regarding that verse. We need to admit, like Peter did after the crucifixion and resurrection, that we were wrong and Christ is right. And that is repentance, a change of mind.

But we also need to repent in terms of verse 18, and that is in terms of direction. We need to move away, or change, or turn around from works of the law to works of faith, from self-righteousness to Christ's righteousness. Now having said this, we have to realize that one of the hardest things for people to do, even Christians, is to repent from self-righteousness. It's one thing repenting from sins, it's another thing to repent of self-righteousness. Let me give you an example.

In one of the discourses that Jesus gave, He made a statement. He said, Luke 11:32:

The men of Nineveh will stand up at the judgment with this generation and condemn it; for they repented at the preaching of Jonah, and now one greater than Jonah is here.

Did Ninevah repent? Yes. What did Ninevah repent of? Of sins. She was guilty of terrible sins. But did the Jews repent? No. And Christ said it would be easier for the Ninevites than for the Jews, because their [Jews] repentance needed to be primarily from self-righteousness. And that is very difficult. So what I want to do is to approach this study from two angles: I want to look at a case study and I want to look at Jesus Christ as our example.

The case study may create a problem in your minds because I'm dealing with a situation that is not the traditional interpretation. So if you disagree with the interpretation, fine, I will not complain, but at least I hope you will get the lesson. I would like to look at a man whose history has been recorded in the Bible, in the oldest book in the Bible. What is the oldest book in the Bible? *Job.* It is believed that Job was written during the 40 years that Moses was in the wilderness.

So please turn to the book of Job. I have wrestled with the book of Job for a long time. I could not see why God allowed Job to be so badly mistreated, and to go through those terrible crises, without a purpose. To me, the purpose of simply proving that he was righteous was not good enough. It did not "jive" in terms of the character of God. Then one day, I was reading *The Desire of Ages*, and I found a statement there — I can't remember the reference so you'll have to look for it — where Ellen G. White said that the history of Job reveals to us, or tells us, that all calamities come from Satan but are allowed by God for a purpose. But she did not say what purpose it was.

So the only way for me to find out was for me to read, and study, and wrestle with the book of Job. And I spent some time with it. I discovered that Job had a problem. At first it was hard for me to accept it, because it was a complete contradiction to what I had understood concerning Job, but I want to expose you to it. You don't have to believe it, but see the conclusion that I came to. Turn to Job chapter one. In the very first verse we are given a statement concerning Job. The second half of the first verse says:

... This man [Job] *was blameless and upright; he feared God and shunned evil.*

Then, in verse 8, the same thing is repeated, but this time in the context of God having a dialogue with Satan. God said to Satan, "Look at my man Job. He is perfect, he is upright, he hates evil, and he fears God":

Then the Lord said to Satan, "Have you considered my servant Job? There is no one on earth like him; he is blameless and upright, a man who fears God and shuns evil."

And you remember what Satan said? "Yes, he does all this because you have built a hedge. You remove the protection and you will see, give him into my hands and you will see what he will do. He will deny You, he will reject you, he will turn his back on you." Verses 9-11:

"Does Job fear God for nothing?" Satan replied. "Have you not put a hedge around him and his household and everything he has? You have blessed the work of his hands, so that his flocks and herds are spread throughout the land. But stretch out your hand and strike everything he has, and he will surely curse you to your face."

And so God said in verse 12a,

The Lord said to Satan, "Very well, then, everything he has is in your hands, but on the man himself do not lay a finger."

"You can have him. All that he has is in your power. But you can't touch him, you can touch his possessions, you can touch what he has, but you can't touch him, you can't kill him."

And so the first test comes, beginning in verse 13 and onwards, there are four calamities, verses 13-18:

One day when Job's sons and daughters were feasting and drinking wine at the oldest brother's house, a messenger came to Job and said, "The men were plowing and the donkeys were grazing nearby, and the Sabeans attacked and carried them off. They put the servants to the sword, and I am the only one who has escaped to tell you!"

While he was still speaking, another messenger came and said, "The fire of God fell from the sky and burned up the sheep and the servants, and I am the only one who has escaped to tell you!"

While he was still speaking, another messenger came and said, "The Chaldeans formed three raiding parties and swept down on your camels and carried them off. They put the servants to the sword, and I am the only one who has escaped to tell you!"

While he was still speaking, yet another messenger came and said, "Your sons and daughters were feasting and drinking wine at the oldest brother's house, when suddenly a mighty wind swept in from the desert and struck the four corners of the house. It collapsed on them and they are dead, and I am the only one who has escaped to tell you!"

Now the four calamities that come to Job, what did Job do, after he went through these four calamities? Job rose up, he tore his robe, which is a typical custom in those days. He shaved his head, which is a typical sign of sorrow. He fell down upon the ground and worshipped and spoke (Verses 20-22):

At this, Job got up and tore his robe and shaved his head. Then he fell to the ground in worship and said: "Naked I came from my mother's womb, and naked I will depart. The Lord gave and the Lord has taken away; may the name of the Lord be praised."

Then, in verse 22:

In all this, Job did not sin by charging God with wrongdoing.

He did not turn his back to God. Now Job was a righteous person. Here is my question: was his righteousness the righteousness of works or was his righteousness the righteousness of faith? Well, let's study it, and we will see the end result. I'm using Job because you will see a very close similarity to the Laodicean message.

God and Satan had a second dialogue in chapter two. Verse 3:

Then the Lord said to Satan, "Have you considered my servant Job? There is no one on earth like him; he is blameless and upright, a man who fears God and shuns evil. And he still maintains his integrity, though you incited me against him to ruin him without any reason."

And Satan said, "Give me him — not his property or his belongings or his children — but I want him in my hands, let me touch him, and you will notice what he will do." Verses 4-5:

"Skin for skin!" Satan replied. "A man will give all he has for his own life. But stretch out your hand and strike his flesh and bones, and he will surely curse you to your face."

And in verse 6 of chapter two the Lord said, "Satan, he is in your hand. The only thing you can't do is kill him." Verse 6:

The Lord said to Satan, "Very well, then, he is in your hands; but you must spare his life."

And what did Satan do? He smote him with boils, terrible boils. Verses 7-8:

So Satan went out from the presence of the Lord and afflicted Job with painful sores from the soles of his feet to the top of his head. Then Job took a piece of broken pottery and scraped himself with it as he sat among the ashes.

And then comes Job's wife in verse 9:

His wife said to him, "Are you still holding on to your integrity?"

Please notice: "Are you still holding on to your righteousness, to your integrity, to your honesty?"

His wife said to him, "Are you still holding on to your integrity? Curse God and die!"

Of course, he rebukes her. Verse 10a:

He replied, "You are talking like a foolish woman. Shall we accept good from God, and not trouble?"

And then the last part of verse 10:

In all this, Job did not sin in what he said.

In a sense, Job passed both the tests. Now comes the three friends. And you will find the names of the three friends in verse 11: Eliphaz, Bildad, and Zophar. Now the arguments of these three friends — so called comforters — is typical of the Eastern mentality and is typical of human mentality. If you read their arguments all through this book — and their argument was wrong, it was not based on truth and, therefore, at the end of the book God rebukes them — they were saying that the reason he was suffering all these calamities plus the boils was because there was some secret sin in his life, that he was doing something behind the backs of the people, and that God was punishing him.

Now does God punish us like that? No, but that was the argument. But I want you to see how Job reacted in this dialogue, and this is important. I will only give you certain texts here and there because we are not able to go through the whole book in detail, but I would recommend that you study for yourselves. In chapter 6, after their arguments were presented and so on, Job responds in verse 24 and you will notice that Job defends his righteousness before his friends:

"Teach me, and I will be quiet; show me where I have been wrong."

"Where have I gone wrong? Show me what is that sin of mine that you are accusing me of." Verse 25:

"How painful are honest words! But what do your arguments prove?"

Verse 30:

"Is there any wickedness on my lips? Can my mouth not discern malice?"

What does Job do? He defends his righteousness. Let's go on to chapter 10, and you will notice that Job is now defending his righteousness even before God. Job 10:2:

"I will say to God: Do not condemn me, but tell me what charges you have against me."

"Come on God, even You, show me where I have gone wrong." Look at verse 7:

"...though you know that I am not guilty..."
Verses 14-15:
If I sinned, you would be watching me and would not let my offense go unpunished. If I am guilty — woe to me! Even if I am innocent, I cannot lift my head, for I am full of shame and drowned in my affliction.

In other words, he's defending himself. "Show me where I'm wrong, show me what my sin is." Go to chapter 13. Job pleads with God to show him his sins. In fact, Job is so confident that he is sinless, look at verses 23-24:

How many wrongs and sins have I committed? Show me my offense and my sin. Why do you hide your face and consider me your enemy?

In other words, "These three 'comforters' are accusing me of some secret sin. God, show me where I'm wrong. I'd like to know."

Was there a sin in Job's life? The answer is no. Was there a problem? Yes, there was a problem, we shall see it in a moment. Chapter 16:15-17:

I have sewed sackcloth over my skin and buried my brow in the dust. My face is red with weeping, deep shadows ring my eyes; yet my hands have been free of violence and my prayer is pure.

Can you see what he's doing? What is he defending? His self-righteousness. Turn to chapter 23 beginning with verse 10. Now all this time there's an argument. These three friends are saying, "There is something wrong, he is defending himself." And Job is saying, "Nothing doing! Let me turn to God and ask Him, let Him show me." Job 23:10-13:

But he knows the way that I take; when he has tested me, I will come forth as gold. My feet have closely followed his steps; I have kept to his way without turning aside. I have not departed from the commands of his lips; I have treasured the words of his mouth more than my daily bread. But he stands alone, and who can oppose him? He does whatever he pleases.

In other words he's saying, "I have not sinned, I have kept His commandments, I have held my integrity." And he goes on. And then the three men come back at him. You need to keep on reading the whole chapter and book.

Then we come to chapter 31, which I recommend you read entirely. Here is the final argument of Job. In the KJV there is a subtitle, "Job's solemn protestation of his integrity." In other words, in this whole chapter Job strongly defends his self-righteousness, and insists that there is no sin in him. And then look at Job 32:1:

So these three men stopped answering Job, because he was righteous in his own eyes.

Tell me, was his righteousness the righteousness of faith, or was it the righteousness of self? Now please, I would like to point out that Job was sincere, he was honest. But there was a problem, a problem that he did not realize; it was subconscious, he did not know. I will show you that in a moment.

After the arguments of the three friends — or comforters, as they are called — a fourth man stepped in. He must have been the youngest of the four because in Job 32:4 it says:

Now Elihu had waited before speaking to Job because they were older than he.

So he was the youngest, he was like Waggoner and Jones, he was a kid, an upstart according to them. And if you read Elihu's argument you will notice that he is trying to convince Job that his problem is not sin, but self-righteousness. Elihu describes Job as saying in Job 34:5,10:

"Job says, 'I am innocent, but God denies me justice.'

"So listen to me, you men of understanding. Far be it from God to do evil, from the Almighty to do wrong."

In other words, God is not punishing me for something that I have done wrong, God is not that kind of a Person. And he's right there. But the question that we must ask is, "Why did God allow Job to go through this terrible experience?" I want to remind you of Hebrews 12:6,11:

...Because the Lord disciplines those he loves, and he punishes everyone he accepts as a son.

No discipline seems pleasant at the time, but painful. Later on, however, it produces a harvest of righteousness and peace for those who have been trained by it.

Now look at Job 35:2, Elihu replies:

"Do you think this is just? You say, 'I will be cleared by God.'"

[Note: Some translations read, "My righteousness is more than God's."]

Boy, Job's self-righteousness is even undermining God's righteousness. The argument goes on until we come to chapter 38. Now in this chapter, God steps in. All this time there has been an argument between Job and his friends, first the three friends and then the fourth friend, Elihu. But now God steps in. And I want you to notice: if you read chapter 38 to the end of the book, you will discover that God rebukes the three men for wrong theology. He says, "You are wrong to say that God punishes because you have done something bad."

And you remember, Christ tried to correct the Jews of the same problem. The Jews believed that if you had leprosy, or you were sick, or you were maimed, or you were born blind, it was because of your sin, or maybe the sin of your parents. Remember, Jesus had to correct this many times in His earthly ministry. And God is correcting the three men. But we are not concerned about that, we are concerned about God's dealing with Job. Job 38:1:

Then the Lord answered Job out of the storm. He said:

Now please don't ask me how He answered by the whirlwind, but that's something which was common in those days. God speaks to Job, and I want you to notice how Job responds. Did Job listen to God? The answer is yes. Did Job repent? The answer is yes. Now look at chapter 40:3-4:

Then Job answered the Lord: "I am unworthy — how can I reply to you? I put my hand over my mouth."

At last Job admits that God is right, that he, Job, is sinful.

The work of the law is to do what? Stop every mouth. Romans 3:19:

Now we know that whatever the law says, it says to those who are under the law, so that every mouth may be silenced and the whole world held accountable to God.

Has the law silenced your mouth?

I am unworthy — how can I reply to you?

"Yes, I answered those three comforters of mine, and I answered Elihu, but how can I answer back to You, God? You are right, I admit it." Job 40:5:

"I spoke once, but I have no answer — twice, but I will say no more."

God, you are always right. In other words, what God is pointing out in Job's life is that there was a problem. That problem was going to hinder his eternal destiny; God had to correct it. He did it by this method, by going through this calamity. Now turn to chapter 42:1-3:

Then Job replied to the Lord: "I know that you can do all things; no plan of yours can be thwarted. You asked, 'Who is this that obscures my counsel without knowledge?' Surely I spoke of things I did not understand, things too wonderful for me to know."

What was he uttering that he understood not? He was defending his self-righteousness. He did not know that his self-righteousness was filthy rags before God. But now God opens his eyes, and Job says, "I have now understood...things too wonderful for me." Verses 4-5:

"You said, 'Listen now, and I will speak; I will question you, and you shall answer me.' My ears had heard of you but now my eyes have seen you."

In other words, "I heard about you before, but now I have direct knowledge from you." Now listen to verse 6, and folks, this is the text that I want you to look at carefully:

"Therefore I despise myself and repent in dust and ashes."

"God, you are right." He's repenting of his self-righteousness. He abhors himself. Have you and I reached that stage? That is why I said that repentance from self-righteousness is very painful, folks, because you have to swallow your pride. You have to swallow your pride as an individual, and we have to swallow our pride as a denomination. It's hard, folks. It was hard for Job, but he realized that God was right. It was hard for Peter to repent about his own opinion. It is hard for us.

But you know the wonderful thing is this: after Job had repented, God said, "The lesson has been learnt, what shall I do?" Look at Job 42:12:

The Lord blessed the latter part of Job's life more than the first.

"I will heap on you, Job, all the blessings now because you have learned your lesson." And then you can read about all that God blessed him with (verses 12-16):

The Lord blessed the latter part of Job's life more than the first. He had fourteen thousand sheep, six thousand camels, a thousand yoke of oxen and a thousand donkeys. And he also had seven sons and three daughters. The first daughter he named Jemimah, the second Keziah and the third Keren-Happuch. Nowhere in all the land were there found women as beautiful as Job's daughters, and their father granted them an inheritance along with their brothers. After this, Job lived a hundred and forty years; he saw his children and their children to the fourth generation.

God blessed him wonderfully. Did God enjoy putting Job through the crisis? No, there was something that had to be learnt and the only way was this method. So God put him through it, but when he had learnt it God blessed him. And the last verse (17) says:

And so he died, old and full of years.

He was a converted man. Folks, that is the condition that we have to reach. We have to abhor ourselves that Christ may be our righteousness. That is why Sister White says, "It is the Counsel to Laodicea that will produce the shaking." That is why she says that there will be many ministers who are not willing to give up their righteousness which is unrighteousness for the pure truth of Christ our Righteousness.

It is hard, folks, because the ultimate end is that a true Christian rejoices in Christ and has no confidence in self. And that is the difficult part. That's why I went briefly through the book of Job to show you that there was a problem. God allowed Satan to touch Job for a purpose. That purpose was to correct him of self-righteousness. Did Job learn from the chastisement? Yes. Did He repent? Yes. I don't know how God is going to chastise us, folks.

He has been rebuking us so far, but it will come, folks, and when it does, you only have to look at the history of Job.

Now I want to read you a statement in this connection. Have you ever wondered why God allows His people, after probation has closed, after God has already declared, "Let him that is righteous remain righteous still...." [By the way, after probation closes, there will be no swapping; those who are righteous by faith will remain so until the end. And those who have rejected Christ will remain in that condition. There is no swapping after probation closes. That's what it means.]

But after probation closes, God is going to allow his children, his people to go through a time of crisis that has never been experienced in the past. Why? Is it simply to prove that He is right? Here's a statement from *The Great Controversy* [by Ellen G. White], and you will notice it's similarity to the story of Job. I'm reading from page 621, talking about "The Time of Trouble":

"Their affliction is great. The flames of the furnace seem about to consume them, but the Refiner will bring them forth as 'gold tried in the fire.'"

Does it sound familiar, those words? Where is she quoting from? The Laodicean Message.

God's love for His children during the period of their severest trial is as strong and tender as in the days of their sunniest prosperity.

So please remember, when you are going through the crisis, it does not mean that God loves you less. That is why I spent so much time in showing you that the love of God never changes, it's eternal, it's agape. But listen to this:

But it is needful for them to be placed in the furnace of fire [It is needful for them to go through this. Why?] that their earthliness might be consumed [And that "earthliness" means simply this problem of self must be consumed] that the image of Christ may be perfectly reflected.

The world desperately needs to see Christ, but it cannot see Christ in you and in me unless the earthliness, until every dross of self has been crucified. And God allows us to go through this.

Now I want to remind you that in the time of trouble the devil will point to you and to your feelings. Will you still feel sinful after probation closes? Yes. Will you feel that you are not good enough to be saved after probation closes? Yes. But the question is, "Who is your righteousness?" Christ. And every dross of self, every earthliness, must be consumed. You must not look at yourself or your experience. Christ can be fully reproduced in you, folks, only when you have completely said good-bye to self.

With this in mind, I want to close by turning to Christ as our example. How was it possible for Christ, not as God, but in His humanity, which I believe was exactly like ours, how was it possible for Christ in His humanity to perfectly reveal his Father? How? Well I want to quickly give you the steps. Turn to Philippians chapter 2, and I want you to look at the admonition that Paul gives us, because Paul is here using Christ as an example. Philippians 2:5:

Your attitude should be the same as that of Christ Jesus:

What kind of mind did Christ have? Okay, if you read the rest of the verses, from 6-8, you will discover that the mind of Christ was a mind that was totally emptied of self. Look at verse 6:

Who, being in very nature God, did not consider equality with God something to be grasped...

By the way, the Greek word, "equality" in this verse means the "absolute sameness" of God. So here Paul is saying that He was one with the Father, He was equal with the Father. So it was not sin for Christ to make Himself equal with the Father,..."But" — there's a "but" beginning in verse 7:

...but made himself nothing, taking the very nature of a servant, being made in human likeness.

The word *kinosis* here ("nothing"), means He emptied Himself, He did not cling to that equality, He totally emptied Himself, He gave up all His divine prerogatives, and He became a slave.

...but made himself nothing, taking the very nature of a servant, being made in human likeness. And being found in appearance as a man, he humbled himself and became obedient to death — even death

on a cross!

You can read the rest on your own but I want to go now and turn to some examples. Please turn your Bibles to the gospel of John. I'm taking just one book. When Jesus emptied Himself of self, Who took over? Was His mind a vacuum? No.

Before we look at John, there is one other passage that I would like to look at. Turn to Luke, because Luke reveals something that we need to know. I want to look at two verses in the book of Luke. First, Luke 4:1:

Jesus, full of the Holy Spirit, returned from the Jordan and was led by the Spirit in the desert,....

How was Jesus led? He was walking now in the Spirit, which is what Paul admonishes the Christian. Look at verse 14, which is after the temptation that He went through and which He passed:

Jesus returned to Galilee in the power of the Spirit, and news about him spread through the whole countryside.

In other words, Jesus emptied Himself, so that it was no longer "I" but the Holy Spirit that controlled Him, and that's why He could reveal the Father. Now turn to John. I want you to notice the mind of Christ, look at John 5:19:

Jesus gave them this answer: "I tell you the truth, the Son can do nothing by himself; he can do only what he sees his Father doing, because whatever the Father does the Son also does."

Remember, Jesus says in John 15, "You can do nothing without me." But Christ Himself said, "I can do nothing of myself." In other words, He was totally God-dependent. Look at verse 30 (John 5:30a):

By myself I can do nothing....

In other words, "Everything I say, everything I do came from God. I was not depending on Myself, I was totally God-dependent." Turn to John 6:57, a very important verse, because not only does Christ tell us how He lived but He also advises us how we should live:

Just as the living Father sent me and I live because of the Father, so the one who feeds on me will live because of me.

In other words, "Just as I was totally dependent on the father, so you must be totally dependent on Me. It is not your righteousness the world needs to see. It is My righteousness."

Turn to John 10; we'll look here at three verses. In this chapter, Jesus claimed that His works originated with the Father, and not with Him. Verse 32:

...But Jesus said to them, "I have shown you many great miracles from the Father. For which of these do you stone me?"

Now I want to remind you in this context, Matthew 5:14, 16:

You are the light of the world. A city on a hill cannot be hidden.

In the same way, let your light shine before men, that they may see your good deeds and praise your Father in heaven.

"You Christians are the light of the world. Let this light so shine that men may see your good works and glorify the Father." In other words, the light shining must be the works of the Father in us, just like in Christ the Father revealed Himself through the works of Christ. So Jesus is saying to the Jews, "Many works have I done which came from the Father, for which one of these are you going to stone Me?" And then in verse 37 and 38 of John 10:

Do not believe me unless I do what my Father does. But if I do it, even though you do not believe me, believe the miracles, that you may know and understand that the Father is in me, and I in the Father.

"I am totally depending on Him, and He is living in Me."

What is Jesus saying here? He is saying, "Look, the works I have done, you can't do, man can't do." Because they were supernatural works that Christ did. "So if you don't believe My words, believe My works." And you remember what Nicodemus said when He came to visit Jesus at night? He said, "You know, nobody could do the works that You are doing unless He comes from God." So Nicodemus at least recognized it.

Now I want to go to John 14 as my last example. In verse 8, Philip says to Jesus:

Philip said, "Lord, show us the Father and that will be enough for us."

Verse 9:

Jesus answered: "Don't you know me, Philip, even after I have been among you such a long time? Anyone who has seen me has seen the Father. How can you say, 'Show us the Father'?"

What did Jesus mean? The answer is found in verses 10 and 11:

"Don't you believe that I am in the Father, and that the Father is in me? The words I say to you are not just my own. Rather, it is the Father, living in me, who is doing his work. Believe me when I say that I am in the Father and the Father is in me; or at least believe on the evidence of the miracles themselves."

In other words, "The message I preach does not come from Me, it comes from the Father."

We must be clear: the same thing is true today. There is a tendency for us in this modern age, because of the tremendous emphasis we put on education and academics, that we present people with our own ideas. That is not feeding, folks. We must allow God to speak through us, otherwise the message becomes meaningless. Verse 11:

"Believe me when I say that I am in the Father and the Father is in me; or at least believe on the evidence of the miracles themselves."

That's very interesting, after Jesus defended His Messiahship through the works that the Father did in Him, He goes on in verse 12, and He says:

"I tell you the truth, anyone who has faith in me will do what I have been doing. He will do even greater things than these, because I am going to the Father."

"The works that I do the believer will do. Why? Because now it is I Who am dwelling by My Spirit in you, and the world needs to see Me in you now."

Can you see what is required of Laodicea? Number one, what is our problem? Is Adventism guilty of gross sins? And the answer is no. Then what is our problem? Self-righteousness, which has deceived us. Do we need to repent of self-righteousness? Yes. It is crucial that we do. And God will go through all lengths, He will rebuke us first, then He will chastise us. How far will He chastise us? I don't know, but looking at Job it can be pretty drastic. How would you like to lose all your kids, all your property, and then be filled with sores? Terrible!

But did God do it out of anger, or out of love? Love. He knew that Job had to learn a lesson, it was for his eternal destiny. And Job did learn the lesson, he did repent, and he abhorred himself. And he said, "God, you are right."

And it is my prayer that we will have the mind of Christ. Christ has given us the best example in having no confidence in the flesh. He did not depend on His humanity for His righteousness, He depended on God. And God worked through Him by the Holy Spirit and the same God wants to work through you.

In concluding, I want to give you a covenant that God wants to make with you, it's called the New Covenant, and that is found in 2 Corinthians 6 and the second half of verse 16:

As God has said: "I will live with them and walk among them, and I will be their God, and they will be my people."

Folks, it is this covenant that God wants to fulfil in our church. And when that happens, the earth will be lightened with God's glory. But that cannot happen until we repent. Repent of what? Of our self-righteousness. And may God help us.

CHAPTER NINE

LAODICEA MUST OPEN THE DOOR

Revelation 3:20:

Here I am! I stand at the door and knock. If anyone hears my voice and opens the door, I will come in and eat with him, and he with me.

I want to remind that you that, in the last two studies, which covered verse 19 of chapter 3, we saw that the greatest need for Laodicea is repentance, to have this change of mind, a change of direction. And, in the context of the Laodicean message, it means two things. First of all, **we need to have a change of mind from our opinion to Christ's opinion.**

Remember in verse 17 what Jesus says about us? We say that we are rich and increased in goods but Christ says that we do not know that we are what? Revelation 3:17:

You say, "I am rich; I have acquired wealth and do not need a thing." But you do not realize that you are wretched, pitiful, poor, blind and naked.

We need to repent over this, we need, like Peter to confess, "God, You are right." We need to confess like Job did at the end of the book, "God you are right, I am vile, I repent in sackcloth and ashes."

The second thing that we need to repent of is in Revelation 3:18: from self-righteousness, which is works of the law, to Christ's righteousness, which is works of faith.

This is one of the hardest things to do. To repent from sins is not too hard. Nineveh had no problem in repenting from sin. But to repent of self-righteousness is extremely hard, because self-righteousness does not look bad outwardly. That is why the Jewish leaders refused to repent; they saw nothing wrong with their self-righteousness. That is why it was such a difficult experience that God had to take Job through before he could confess that there was nothing good in him.

Now some of you may ask the question, "How can we tell, what is Christ's righteousness and what is self-righteousness?" Well, it's very hard, you can't tell easily. But the thing is you must always have the attitude in your mind that there is nothing good in me, that God deserves all the praise, all the glory, there is to be no boasting, inwardly or outwardly.

But now the question is, "How is the repentance to be realized? What does God expect from us?" And that is what we will cover today, verse 20. So look at Revelation 3:20:

Here I am! I stand at the door and knock. If anyone hears my voice and opens the door, I will come in and eat with him, and he with me.

Now, this expression of "knocking on the door" and wanting "to come in" is taken from the book written by Solomon, "Song of Songs." Most Christians have great difficulty with the Song of Songs, some even think it's pornography, Biblical pornography. I would recommend to you a book that to me is the finest book I've ever read concerning the Song of Songs; it gives us a tremendous spiritual application. It is by a Chinese author, some of you are familiar with him, by the name of Watchman Nee. He has written a book on the Song of Songs, and just go to a Christian book store and ask them to get the book for you if you don't have it. It's an excellent book on the Song of Songs. Because the Song of Songs is written really for the spiritually minded people, it is God's concern to have a close fellowship with His believers. And that is what Christ is pleading for.

Now the first thing I want you to take note of is the first expression or word, "Here I am!" ("Behold" in some translations).

It's a very interesting expression. It means, "Please become aware of" or "take notice." Take notice of what?

If you look at the next statement, "I stand at the door and knock," it sounds as if Christ is outside of you, and if He's outside of you, it means that you're unconverted. So the question is, "Is Christ talking here to unconverted people?" And the answer is no, because He already identifies with Laodicea as His people. What He means is, "I am outside of your works," because that's the issue. "I know your works, I am not the Source of your works, it's your self-righteousness that you're doing. And I want to be inside. I want to be the Source of your works, I want to be part of your works." In other words, "I'm knocking to be the Source of your works. Please let Me be your righteousness. Not only in terms of your standing before God, but in terms of your Christian living."

Now to understand this we need to realize that the New Testament divides Christians into two camps. And I want to give you a passage. Turn to 1 Corinthians. This is a problem that we need to come to grips with. I want you to notice what Paul does here, he divides Christians into two camps, 1 Corinthians 3:1-3:

Brothers, I could not address you as spiritual but as worldly...

So there are two kinds of Christians: spiritual and carnal. Now I want you to notice how he defines the carnal Christian. He doesn't say, "the unconverted," he says:

...mere infants in Christ....

They're babies in Christ. Do babies walk perfectly, or do they fall down? Why do they fall down? Because they're babies, they're weak, you see? Okay, infants in Christ....

...I gave you milk...

This is number two, there are two problems with babies. Number one you can't give them heavy stuff, you can't give them "linkettes," you know. When we were in the mission field we used to take Loma Linda stuff as a treat. Once in a blue moon we would open a can, and I remember the first time we opened a can of sliced chicken, you know this Loma Linda [meatless] chicken. And we gave a little bit to our daughter who was just learning to eat solid foods. And she chewed, and she chewed, and she chewed and she couldn't swallow the thing. And she said, "This is terrible stuff!"

And I said, "Well, yes ... it's plastic you know, and there is difficulty swallowing it." Now they have improved it since then, it was very fibery, it was stringy. She couldn't disintegrate the stuff and swallow it. Finally she had to throw it on the floor and the cat enjoyed it. So it was pretty good, at least the cat thought so. And Paul is saying:

...I gave you milk, not solid food, for you were not yet ready for it. Indeed, you are still not ready. You are still worldly.

Now Paul wrote Corinthians, this letter, approximately 10 years after the Corinthian church was established. In other words, "You have not grown spiritually, you are still worldly." And the evidence is this:

For since there is jealousy and quarreling among you, are you not worldly? Are you not acting like mere men?

In other words, your behaviour is not like a Christian. Your behaviour is like the worldly people. He doesn't say that they are lost; in fact, in verse 16:

Don't you know that you yourselves are God's temple and that God's Spirit lives in you?

So they are converted. Now please don't tell me, that when Paul wrote the first three verses they were unconverted like one person told me, but when he came to verse 16 they were converted. That is a terrible exegesis, because I'll take you to chapter 4 and chapter 5 and chapter 6 and there he's rebuking them for their behaviour.

But let me give you the spiritual Christian. The spiritual Christian is not only one that is converted, but who is walking in the Spirit. Now what is the distinction between a carnal Christian and a spiritual Christian? The issue is not conversion here. The issue is that a carnal Christian is primarily walking in the flesh. And the result is this, because he's dominated by self, that is what the flesh is, there are two problems with him:

1. He is a poor witness.

2.   He misrepresents Christ.

When people look at him they say, "Boy, if this is Christianity, I want nothing to do with it." He's a very poor representative of Christ. And I'll be frank with you, it is because of poor witnessing that the Eastern European block went Marxist. They were all Christian countries, why did they turn Marxist? Because the Christian church failed to reveal the life of Christ. And it failed because the believers were worldly Christians, on the whole. But there is a third point I need to bring up about worldly Christians. Worldly Christians are in a very dangerous condition. It is very easy for the Devil to pull them out of Christ, because they are already walking in the flesh. Now when you look at a worldly Christian, and when you look at the people of the world, there is very little difference in behaviour. And that is why we must not judge. It is hard to judge whether a worldly Christian is converted or unconverted, because in behaviour he is no different from the people of the world.

Okay, I want to give you two examples of what happens when you are a Christian that is spiritual. A spiritual Christian is not only converted, but he is walking in the Spirit. Such a believer can be described as the light of the world, because he's reflecting Jesus Christ. And when this happens two things will take place:

1.   These people will subdue the flesh through the power of the Spirit.
2.   They will reflect the righteousness of Christ.

I want to give you two examples, turn to Galatians 5, and I want you to notice what Paul says in verses 16-18. This is admonishment that Paul is giving to believers:

So I say, live by the Spirit, and you will not gratify the desires of the sinful nature. For the sinful nature desires what is contrary to the Spirit, and the Spirit what is contrary to the sinful nature. They are in conflict with each other, so that you do not do what you want. But if you are led by the Spirit, you are not under law.

In other words, the only way to conquer the flesh is not by willpower, or by trying, but by walking in the Spirit. You'll have another statement made by Paul in Romans 13:14 where he says:

Rather, clothe yourselves with the Lord Jesus Christ, and do not think about how to gratify the desires of the sinful nature.

So one of the evidences of a spiritual Christian is that through the power of the indwelling Spirit the flesh is subdued. And by the way, you have to read Galatians 5:17-18 only in the context of verse 16 because verses 17 and 18 are explanations of that statement he makes in verse 16. But I want to go to Galatians 5:22-23 and there Paul tells us that when we walk in the Spirit:

But the fruit of the Spirit is love, joy, peace, patience, kindness, goodness, faithfulness, gentleness and self-control. Against such things there is no law.

In other words, this is in harmony with the law.

Now, in order to appreciate this, what we need to understand is that imparted righteousness takes place only when we have lost all confidence in the flesh and we can say in our hearts, "Not I, but Christ."

So I'm going to take you through four stages, because there is a lot of confusion in this area, and I'm going to use Adam as a type or example. I'm going to look at Adam before the fall, I'm going to look at Adam after the fall, I'm going to look at Adam after his conversion, and I'm going to look at Adam when Christ comes the second time. There are four stages. Please turn to 1 Thessalonians chapter 5. In 1 Thessalonians 5:23 Paul is praying concerning the believers in Thessalonica, and he says:

May God himself, the God of peace, sanctify you through and through. May your whole spirit, soul and body be kept blameless at the coming of our Lord Jesus Christ.

He breaks up man into three elements. Now the first thing I would like to say is that none of these three elements are capable of independent existence. That's the heresy of "the immortal soul." All these three elements together make up the human being, but when you die, all three come to an end, folks; nothing exists beyond that. I can give you many texts where the Bible teaches the body, soul, and spirit.

If you think of these three elements as one inside the other, the **spirit** is the inmost circle. That is the **dwelling place of God**. In fact, if you read *Desire of Ages*, page 161, you will find that there Ellen G. White says that,

"...from eternal ages it was God's purpose that every created being, from the bright and holy angels, the seraphs, to men, should be a temple for the indwelling of the Creator."

In other words, God created man that He may indwell in man. When God created Adam, Adam was indwelt by the Holy Spirit.

By the way, the essence of our spirit is the conscience. It is through the conscience that God directs you. The **soul** is the **human mind**, of course, the center being the will. So it is in the soul that we make decisions. And the **body**, of course, is the outward, physical body. By the way, you will notice these three elements are very closely related to the sanctuary. Remember, the sanctuary is a type not only of Christ but of the believer. The Most Holy Place, which represents the Spirit, is where God dwells. The Holy Place is where God functions, the priest functioned in the Holy Place. And of course the courtyard, which is the body is where the sacrifice took place. Please remember what Paul says in Romans 12:1:

Therefore, I urge you, brothers, in view of God's mercy, to offer your bodies as living sacrifices, holy and pleasing to God — this is your spiritual act of worship.

There are three things that I want to say about Adam at creation:

1. Adam was totally God dependent, and that, by the way, was the meaning of the Sabbath Covenant. "You must depend on Me totally." That is why we must never present the Sabbath as the seventh day of man, it's the seventh day of God. It was the first day of man. Man did not begin by working, he began by resting in God's provision. God worked first, and then He rested. He rested because His work was perfect and finished. Man did not

begin with the same method. Man began with resting in God. And then, the six days he enjoyed what God created, what he had received by faith. So please remember that Adam was totally dependent. The moment that he sinned, God said to him, "From now onward, you will earn your bread by your sweat, because you have turned your back to me."

2. There was perfect harmony between the Divine and the human nature. There was never a struggle in Adam, between his human nature and the Holy Spirit that dwelt in him. They were in perfect harmony, because Adam was created in the image of God.

3. The Spirit, which was the source of God's love, controlled him. Which means that the soul and the body of Adam were totally controlled by God's Spirit, which means that his humanity reflected the glory of God, the love of God. He did not even need any clothing; the reflection of God was through his body. He revealed the character of God.

That is Adam before the fall. What happened to Adam when he sinned? We need to know number two because that is how you and I were born.

1. Adam's sin was turning his back to God, so the Holy Spirit left him. And so he died — he died spiritually, not physically. And self took the place of the Holy Spirit. So at the very heart of fallen man is self. In Adam, the love was turned inwardly, towards himself, and that is what *eros* is, it's a U-turn *agape*. So number one, when Adam sinned, he turned from God to self.

2. He died spiritually. By the way, Ephesians 2:1 (and verse 5) tells us that we are born spiritually dead:

As for you, you were dead in your transgressions and sins....

1. Self-love, which is *eros*, replaced God's divine love, which is Agape. So we do possess the capacity to love, but that love is self-

centered.

2. The human life came under the curse of the law. That means that Adam had no right legally to live any longer. He was condemned.

3. The human nature became a slave to sin. That is what the Bible means by the word "worldly" (or "carnal"). Adam's life became sinful.

Now, this is Adam at the fall; this is how you and I are born. We are born carnal (or worldly); we are born dominated by self; we are born slaves to sin. And there is nothing that you and I can do to save ourselves, because it is impossible. It is like a farmer trying to produce apples from orange trees: impossible. The Bible is very clear (Jeremiah 13:23):

Can the Ethiopian change his skin or the leopard its spots? Neither can you do good who are accustomed to doing evil.

They try, they put a little makeup, you know. It's very interesting. In Africa, the women are always trying to straighten their hair. In America, the women are always trying to curl their hair. Mankind is never satisfied. But you can't do it, you can do it for a season, but you have to go to the hairdresser over and over again and it becomes a very expensive procedure. Am I correct? The poor husbands have to pay it sometimes, unless the wife is working.

What happens when a person is converted? What change takes place in the person?

1. Conversion means accepting Christ as your life. The first thing that takes place when you are converted is that the Holy Spirit comes and dwells in your spirit. Just like Adam before the fall the Holy Spirit dwells in you. This is because you have surrendered your life to the cross, and you have accepted the formula of the gospel, which is, "Not I, but Christ."

2. Paul tells us that this means that you have been made spiritually alive. By birth, because of the fall, you were born spiritually dead, but now you have become spiritually alive.

3. Because you have accepted Christ as your Saviour and as your Righteousness, you stand justified before the law. So now the issue of whether you'll make it to heaven is no longer there. As far as God is concerned, He looks at you as you are in His Son.

4. But, and this point is very important, your human nature has not changed one iota. It is still carnal. Which means that your human nature is still controlled by self. And because of this, there is a conflict that takes place in you. The conflict is between the Divine Nature, which through the Holy Spirit is dwelling in you, and the human nature which is still enmity with God. And these two, folks, are in conflict all the time. And many Christians are confused about this, because they think that this conflict means that they are not converted. This is not true, folks. In fact, if you don't have the conflict, then I question your conversion. The conflict is a good sign, because it's telling you that now, your mind has repented, but your nature hasn't, and there is a conflict.

Now where does the conflict take place? Now here's the problem, the Spirit that dwells in you cannot produce any righteousness (I'm now talking about imparted righteousness) the Spirit that dwells in you cannot impart righteousness to you through your works, without the consent off the will. The Holy Spirit will never do work by compulsion. He can do it, but He will not because God has created us as free moral agents.

The body cannot fulfill its desires for sin without the consent of the will. So the battle ground in the Christian is the human mind. It's in your mind, in your thoughts, your desires that there is a constant battle. Am I talking about something that you are all familiar with? Yes. The mind is always struggling. And by the way, I believe Romans 7 is describing that struggle. With the mind, you want to do the law of God. The flesh wants to do the law of sin. And this struggle is constant.

Now when does this struggle stop? Well, I have bad news, it does not stop until the second coming of Christ, or until this body dies.

Then the mind dies with it and there is no more struggle. So there is no way that you can say, "I have graduated from the struggle." Now I'm not talking about getting victory, I'm talking about the struggle.

Now the question: "Can the mind conquer the flesh?" And the answer is no. It can defy the flesh, but can never conquer it. What do I mean by defy? Well, let's say you have attended a week of prayer, you have been stirred up and you make resolutions: "From now onwards, I am not going to have any dessert after meals." Have you ever made that resolution? "No more desserts for me!" Well, you succeed the first day, the second day, the third day, and then the fourth day you have been working extremely hard and you are tired, and then your wife has brought some wonderful cookies made for you, and you look at it and your mouth waters, and you say, "Boy, just one." And before you know it, it's all gone.

I once received a card in the mail from the Holts family — Russel Holts and his wife. We had given these friends a cookie jar as a gift. And the wife says, "I don't know what's wrong. Every time I put cookies in there, presto! They disappear." That's the flesh, folks; you can't avoid it. I have the same problem, so my wife has to hide the cookies.

Of course, some of you will say, "But I have overcome the cookies." Yes, you may have overcome the cookies, but there's something else that you haven't overcome that I have overcome, too. So please, before you point your finger at me, I can point my finger at you. We all have our own problems. To some it's cookies, to others it's something else. I don't know what your problem is. Some people have no problem getting up in the morning. But for some people, boy, it's the greatest problem to get up in the morning. Some people have no problem in going to bed at night. Other people, they can't, they have to wait and wait because they can't sleep. So we all have our problems.

But the thing is, the human mind cannot conquer the flesh. Romans 7 makes it clear. Can the Spirit conquer the flesh? I want to give you a text, Romans 8, look at verse 2:

...Because through Christ Jesus the law of the Spirit of life set me free from the law of sin and death.

Now the word "law" appears twice here. And it is used in terms of a force. Just like we have the law of gravity; the law of gravity is a force. The first thing I would like to say about Romans 8:2 is that Paul is not talking about the Christian experience, he is talking about a truth that took place in Christ. He says that there were two forces that met in Christ:

1. The law of sin, and
2. The law of the Spirit.

Now where is the law of sin residing? Well, he has explained it in Romans 7. Look at verses 22 and 23:

For in my inner being I delight in God's law; but I see another law at work in the members of my body, waging war against the law of my mind and making me a prisoner of the law of sin at work within my members.

"In my converted mind and spirit, I want to keep the law of God. But my members...!"

What does he mean by "members"? He doesn't mean church members. He means, "My body, my hands and feet and so on" or "in my human nature, in my flesh."

...But I see another law at work in the members of my body, waging war against the law of my mind and making me a prisoner of the law of sin at work within my members.

Now please remember that he's explaining what he says in verse 18. What does he say in verse 18?

I know that nothing good lives in me, that is, in my sinful nature. For I have the desire to do what is good [I can choose in my mind to obey God], *but I cannot carry it out.*

And then he explains that the reason that he cannot do the will of his mind is because there is a flesh that is opposing him, the law of sin. This law of sin and the law of the Spirit met together in Jesus Christ. And Who won, the Spirit or the flesh? Now please remember the word, "law" not only means a force, but a "constant force." You see, the will is not a constant force. It is a force, but not constant. Sometimes my will is strong, sometimes it is weak. That is not true with the law of sin; it is constant all the time. And so is the law of the spirit: constant. But they are opposite forces. One is towards sin, one is towards righteousness. In Christ these two laws met and Who won? Well, in Romans 8:3 I read that Jesus Christ condemned sin. Where? In the flesh. He condemned the law of sin in the flesh, because that's the context. Romans 8:3:

For what the law was powerless to do in that it was weakened by the sinful nature, God did by sending his own Son in the likeness of sinful man to be a sin offering. And so he condemned sin in sinful man,...

Now He did it for two reasons. Number one, He did it to justify us. Because I'll tell you, folks, it is not only your acts that condemn you, your very sinful nature condemns you. "This flesh and blood cannot inherit the kingdom of God." So Christ did not only deal with my acts, he dealt with what I am. And on the cross, He executed not only my sins, but the "law of sin" in my flesh.

But there was another reason. Christ condemned sin in the flesh not only to justify me, but look at verse 4:

...in order that the righteous requirements of the law might be fully met in us, who do not live according to the sinful nature but according to the Spirit.

In other words, if you walk after the Spirit, that same Spirit, the law of the Spirit, will set you free in experience from the law of sin, but please remember, not to save you but to give evidence. In other words, what Christ is saying to Laodicea is, "I want to be the source of your Christian living. Stop trying to be good, you will never make it. I want to come in and dwell in you, and walk in you." In other words, the Laodicean plea that Christ is making to the church is found in the new covenant promise, and so please turn to 2 Corinthians 6:16:

What agreement is there between the temple of God and idols? For we are the temple of the living God. As God has said: "I will live with them and walk among them, and I will be their God, and they will be my people."

And by the way, He dwells in every believer, every converted Christian has the Holy Spirit dwelling within, both the carnal and the spiritual Christian have God dwelling in them. But God wants to do two things:

1. Dwell in them.
2. Walk in them.

Is God walking in the carnal Christian? The answer is no. Therefore, the carnal Christian is a misrepresentation of Christ. And God wants Laodicea to be spiritual. The only way we can become spiritual and allow God to walk in us is by saying, "Not I, but Christ." And that is painful for the self-righteous.

Now having said this, I want now to look at the two choices that are left with us. In other words, when a person is unconverted, this is the unconverted man: he has only one life to control him, the life of the flesh. In other words, the unbeliever can only walk in the flesh, because that's all he has, and that's all he is. The believer has two things: (1) He is flesh — he still has the carnal flesh, but he also has (2) the Spirit. So there are two possibilities with the believer: he can either walk in the flesh or he can walk in the spirit. If you turn to Romans 8, you will notice that after he has explained the truth as it is in Christ, he's admonishing the believers in Rome not to walk in the flesh. For example, look at Romans 8:12. First of all, he reminds them, in verse 9a:

You, however, are controlled not by the sinful nature but by the Spirit, if the Spirit of God lives in you.

And then he goes on to prove that if he doesn't dwell in you, you're unconverted. But now look at verse 11:

And if the Spirit of him who raised Jesus from the dead is living in you, he who raised Christ from the dead will also give life to your mortal bodies through his Spirit, who lives in you.

In other words, it is only the Spirit that can produce righteousness. It is only the Spirit that can conquer the flesh. You can't! You cannot.

Now why does Paul use the idea of resurrection? Because, please remember, the ultimate power of sin is to put you in the grave. Have you conquered the grave? If you have, then you can conquer the flesh. But if you haven't conquered the grave, you can't conquer the flesh.

Has Christ conquered the grave? Yes. That was the greatest evidence. How did He conquer the grave? By His power, or by the power of the Spirit? And Paul says here, "Just like the Spirit proved His power by raising Christ from the dead, so also if you are walking in the Spirit He will be able to mortify or subdue the flesh and produce righteousness in you." Romans 8:12-13:

Therefore, brothers, we have an obligation — but it is not to the sinful nature, to live according to it. For if you live according to the sinful nature, you will die; but if by the Spirit you put to death the misdeeds of the body, you will live....

Now what is Paul saying here? Paul is saying that if you allow the flesh to control you, ultimately the flesh will pull you out of Christ and you will die. Because I'll tell you, when you walk in the flesh, you are doing something to the Spirit. Do you know what you're doing? Let me give you the text: Ephesians 4:30. And by the way, Ephesians 4:30 is talking in the context of Christian living. Let me read a few verses before and after. Okay, let's start with verse 25 of Ephesians 4, through verse 30:

Therefore each of you must put off falsehood and speak truthfully to his neighbor, for we are all members of one body. "In your anger do not sin": Do not let the sun go down while you are still angry, and do not give the devil a foothold. He who has been stealing must steal no longer, but must work, doing something useful with his own hands, that he may have something to share with those in need.

Do not let any unwholesome talk come out of your mouths, but only what is helpful for building others up according to their needs, that it may benefit those who listen. [Verse 30]: And do not grieve the Holy Spirit of God, with whom you were sealed for the day of redemption.

Now please, what Paul is saying here, is that as long as the Spirit of God dwells in you, you are sealed in terms of your eternal salvation. But don't grieve Him, because there is a possibility for you to say to the Holy Spirit, "I don't want You any more." It is possible to grieve the Holy Spirit to the point where He will leave you. And when that happens, folks, you are now no longer under the umbrella of justification by faith. You have said good-bye to it.

As a Christian, you have two possibilities: (1) you can walk in the Spirit, because the Spirit dwells in you, or (2) you can walk in the flesh, which is your natural life. And there is always a conflict between these two. Both want your mind. Because the flesh cannot fulfil sin without the mind and the Spirit cannot fulfil His desires without the mind. And so this constant struggle makes life quite miserable for us sometimes. What does this do? It begins to make you groan. Are you groaning because of the flesh? Well I have some good news for you. Turn to Romans 8, where Paul is discussing this. And he says in verses 22-23, after explaining about creation, he says:

We know that the whole creation has been groaning as in the pains of childbirth right up to the present time. Not only so, but we ourselves, who have the firstfruits of the Spirit, groan inwardly as we wait eagerly for our adoption as sons, the redemption of our bodies.

Is this groaning going to go on forever? The answer is no. We will have to groan until when? Verses 24-25:

For in this hope we were saved. But hope that is seen is no hope at all. Who hopes for what he already has? But if we hope for what we do not yet have, we wait for it patiently.

Folks, the groaning will take place until the second coming of Christ. There will never come a time when your flesh will say, "I give up. I will not give you any more trouble." I hate to say this, the flesh will not give up. And so, there is this constant struggle. Can the flesh be conquered? Yes. Not by you, not by your will, but by the Spirit. And it will only do it as you walk in the Spirit. And Christ is saying, "Let me come, to not only dwell with you, but let Me sup with you, and you with Me. Let me totally identify Myself with you." That's the meaning of "sup with you, and you with Me."

God wants to take over, He wants to control your body, He wants to control your mind. But He will never do it by compulsion. That is why Sister White says that there is a very important part for us to do, our wills must be submitted to the will of God. And that, folks, is the cross. You remember Gethsemane? The flesh of cross did not want to die. What did Jesus say to His father? Luke 22:42:

"Father, if you are willing, take this cup from me; yet not my will, but yours be done."

And this is the thing that you have to say constantly.

So what is Jesus crying, what is He pleading with Laodicea? He's saying, "I want to come, not only to dwell with you, because I'm already doing that, but I want to walk in you. Would you please allow Me to walk in You? What you are doing may appear very nice to you, but it is polluted with self. It's only when I'm walking in you that the righteousness that is produced in you is really true righteousness."

And so, folks, there is this great concern. There is, number one, when you walk in the flesh, there is a danger that the devil will pull you out of Christ. And number two, when you walk in the flesh, we can never fully represent Christ. We are a bad witness to the world. And the crying need, folks, is for the Christian church to reveal to the world the power of the gospel in their lives.

We are saved, we are sealed unto the day of redemption, but are we being a witness for Christ, or are we walking like men? That's the question. And it is my prayer folks, that we will be willing to repent of our self-righteousness, and let Christ come in and walk in us, and let the world see, not me, But Him. And so we can say with Paul (Galatians 2:20):

I have been crucified with Christ and I no longer live, but Christ lives in me. The life I live in the body, I live by faith in the Son of God, who loved me and gave himself for me.

When this happens, folks, the earth will be lightened with His glory, and we will have overcome, which is verse 21: "To him who overcomes...." And so our next study will be Revelation 3:21:

To him who overcomes, I will give the right to sit with me on my throne, just as I overcame and sat down with my Father on his throne.

CHAPTER TEN

LAODICEA MUST OVERCOME

Revelation 3:21:

To him who overcomes, I will give the right to sit with me on my throne, just as I overcame and sat down with my Father on his throne.

The ultimate purpose of the messages to the seven churches is that God's people may overcome. When you read the seven messages of Revelation, you will notice that there are two phrases that are applied to all the seven messages. Each of them begins with the phrase "I know your deeds" ("I know thy works," in some translations) because it's an evaluation of God's people through history. And they all end up with this:

To him who overcomes....

The word "overcomes" means "he that is victorious." I would like to read verse 21 from the Philips translation. I don't know how many of you have the Philips, it's a good paraphrase, he's done a good job and makes things much easier. Let me read Revelation 3:21-22 from the Philips:

As for the victorious, I will give him the honour of sitting beside Me on My throne, just as I Myself have won the victory and have taken My seat beside My Father on His throne. Let the listener hear what the Spirit says to the churches.

Now the question we want to ask this evening is, "In what sense must Laodicea overcome?" I want us to analyze this passage because it is very relevant to our study of the Laodicean message which is "Christ our righteousness."

Christ tells us that He wants us to overcome, and the question is, "Overcome what?" And we will see, folks, that the heart of the message is that we need to overcome *self*. Because at the heart of our problem, whether it's law-keeping or whether it's righteousness by self, the heart of the problem is self. Where you have self, you have a problem. And I want you to notice that what Christ is saying here is that those who overcome...

...I will give the right to sit with me on my throne, just as I overcame ...

Please notice, Christ is not dealing here with salvation, but with a privilege. If you look in the New Testament, you will see that it alludes to two groups that will be in heaven. There will be the bride and there will be the guests. There will be those who will serve Him in the temple and there will be the rest. And I want to give you some texts, because, you see, all who are in heaven will have by faith received the imputed righteousness of Christ. There will be nobody in heaven without the imputed righteousness of Christ. Because that qualifies us for heaven.

But the ones who are special are those who by faith have experienced the righteousness of Christ which is what we call the "imparted" righteousness of Christ. And I want to give you some texts, because this is the basic desire of Jesus Christ. Please turn first of all to Revelation 19, and we will look at a couple of verses here. Look at verses 7 through 9. This is talking about the last generation of Christians. This chapter is discussing the marriage of the Lamb.

"Let us rejoice and be glad and give him glory! For the wedding of the Lamb has come, and his bride has made herself ready. Fine linen, bright and clean, was given her to wear." (Fine linen stands for the righteous acts of the saints.)

Then the angel said to me, "Write: 'Blessed are those who are invited to the wedding supper of the Lamb!'" And he added, "These are the true words of God."

So please remember there is the bride and there are the guests. Turn to chapter 14 of Revelation, and the other two verses that I am giving you are dealing with the 144,000 which we are going to cover the next two studies. Revelation 14:2-5:

And I heard a sound from heaven like the roar of rushing waters and like a loud peal of thunder. The sound I heard was like that of harpists playing their harps. And they sang a new song before the throne and before the four living creatures and the elders. No one [remember, this is in heaven] *could learn the song except the 144,000 who had been redeemed from the earth. These are those who did not defile themselves with women, for they kept themselves pure. They follow the Lamb wherever he goes. They were purchased from among men and offered as firstfruits to God and the Lamb. No lie was found in their mouths; they are blameless.*

This is a special group, distinct from the rest. Only the 144,000. And we will deal with the 144,000 the next two studies. Now what's so special about them?

...The 144,000 who had been redeemed from the earth. These are those who did not defile themselves with women, for they kept themselves pure. They follow the Lamb wherever he goes. They were purchased from among men and offered as firstfruits to God and the Lamb.

They are the ones who have experienced the full power of the gospel. They have not only been saved by faith, but they have experienced the power of the gospel. And in verse 5:

No lie was found in their mouths; they are blameless.

And then the next one is chapter 7 of Revelation, and look at verses 14 and 15. The question is asked, "Who are these people?" We'll start with that question in verse 13:

Then one of the elders asked me, "These in white robes — who are they, and where did they come from?"

I answered, "Sir, you know."

And he said, "These are they who have come out of the great tribulation; they have washed their robes and made them white in the blood of the Lamb. [These are they who have experienced the power of the cross.] *Therefore, they are before the throne of God and serve him day and night in his temple; and he who sits on the throne will spread his tent over them."*

So this is the privilege that God wants to give each one of us. Now why am I giving you these texts? Well, go back to Revelation 3, and I want you to notice something here that is not true with the other six messages. As I mentioned all six messages end up with "To him who overcomes." But in the seventh church, we read one step further. We have to overcome, "just as Christ overcame."

So God wants the last generation of Christians to overcome even as He overcame. So we need to look at Christ now as our example. What did He overcome? Now please remember that this is a desire that God has for all believers. But what did Christ overcome? I want to give you several things. First of all, He overcame the world. Turn to John 16 and listen to what Jesus says to His disciples in verse 33:

"I have told you these things, so that in me you may have peace. [Please notice, we have peace only in Christ, never in ourselves.] *In this world you will have trouble. But take heart! I have overcome the world."*

Now what did Christ mean when He said, "I have overcome the world"? First of all, He means that He overcame the prince of this world. You will find that in John 14:30:

I will not speak with you much longer, for the prince of this world is coming. He has no hold on me,....

Jesus totally overcame the evil one. And please remember, He overcame the evil one on our behalf. So, in Christ, we have that wonderful hope. The other thing that He overcame by the word "world" is found in 1 John 2:16. Jesus overcame this, also. What does the Bible link the world with?

For everything in the world — the cravings of sinful man, the lust of his eyes and the boasting of what he has and does — comes not from the Father but from the world.

Some translations list these as "the lust of the flesh, the lust of the eyes, and the pride of life."

And Christ overcame this. He overcame the devil, He overcame the flesh, and He overcame the law of sin in the members. Romans 8:3 tells us that He condemned sin in the flesh:

For what the law was powerless to do in that it was weakened by the sinful nature, God did by sending his own Son in the likeness of sinful man to be a sin offering. And so he condemned sin in sinful man,....

It means He condemned the law of sin, or the principle of sin, which is the principle of self. We already saw that this is the stumbling block to all that we have to fight within this Christian living.

Why did Christ overcome the devil, why did he overcome the flesh, why did he overcome self? That He may *impart* this victory to us. We must be clear that Christ did not do this thing only for our benefit, but for our experience. I want to give you now some texts. First of all, turn to Luke 10:19, and see what Christ says here:

I have given you authority to trample on snakes and scorpions and to overcome all the power of the enemy [the enemy is the devil]; *nothing will harm you.*

Now of course, He did not mean only literal snakes, but serpents represent Satan and His angels.

Does the devil accuse you? Yes. Revelation 12:10 says he is "the accuser of our brothers."

Then I heard a loud voice in heaven say: "Now have come the salvation and the power and the kingdom of our God, and the authority of his Christ. For the accuser of our brothers, who accuses them before our God day and night, has been hurled down."

When he knocks you down with his accusations, what do you do? Do you lie down? Or do you overcome his accusations by the blood of the Lamb, which is verse 11:

They overcame him by the blood of the Lamb and by the word of their testimony; they did not love their lives so much as to shrink from death.

Please remember that Christ overcame the devil that you might overcome the devil. And he comes to us through our conscience, he comes to us through many ways and he points his finger at you and he says, "You are not good enough to be saved, you don't deserve to go to heaven." Is he right? Yes. "But now the righteousness of God..." — this is what we can say to the devil. So, you see, we have power through Jesus Christ.

Okay, turn now to Galatians 1:4, and see what Paul tells us here that Christ has brought to us through His redemptive work:

...Who gave himself for our sins to rescue us from the present evil age, according to the will of our God and Father,....

Please notice, through Christ, we have deliverance from this present evil world. And that's why, folks, we have a hope. Our home is not in this world forever. We are delivered from it, and we are delivered from the evil of this world. I want to give one more text in this connection. Turn to 1 John 5:4, and notice what John says, something very similar to what we just read in Galatians:

...For everyone born of God overcomes the world. This is the victory that has overcome the world, even our faith.

How do we overcome the world? Remember, the word, "overcome" and the word, "victorious" are synonymous.

...For everyone born of God overcomes the world. This is the victory that has overcome the world, even our faith.

Please don't think that you can overcome the world by your willpower. It's by faith, folks. Now what does he mean by overcoming the world? We saw in 1 John 2:16:

For everything in the world — the cravings of sinful man, the lust of his eyes and the boasting of what he has and does — comes not from the Father but from the world.

Now let's go to Romans 8. I mentioned Romans 8:3 in terms of what Christ did. Paul has already explained to us in Romans 7, beginning in verse 15, that in and of ourselves we cannot keep the law. In fact, that's how he ends chapter 7. Romans 7:15-25:

I do not understand what I do. For what I want to do I do not do, but what I hate I do. And if I do what I do not want to do, I agree that the law is good. As it is, it is no longer I myself who do it, but it is sin living in me. I know that nothing good lives in me, that is, in my sinful nature. For I have the desire to do what is good, but I cannot carry it out. For

what I do is not the good I want to do; no, the evil I do not want to do —
this I keep on doing. Now if I do what I do not want to do, it is no longer
I who do it, but it is sin living in me that does it.

So I find this law at work: When I want to do good, evil is right there
with me. For in my inner being I delight in God's law; but I see another
law at work in the members of my body, waging war against the law
of my mind and making me a prisoner of the law of sin at work within
my members. What a wretched man I am! Who will rescue me from
this body of death? Thanks be to God — through Jesus Christ our Lord!
So then, I myself in my mind am a slave to God's law, but in the sinful
nature a slave to the law of sin.

"I myself in my mind am a slave to God's law, but in the sinful
nature a slave to the law of sin."

And if you were to put your converted mind and your flesh
together in battle, which is what happens in your life, who will win?
Can your mind conquer the flesh? And the answer is, "No." It can
defy the flesh for a time, but it can't conquer it. But now we are told
in Romans 8:3, the next chapter, that Christ condemned this law of
sin in the flesh. Why? Look at that and verse 4 now:

For what the law was powerless to do in that it was weakened by the
sinful nature, God did by sending his own Son in the likeness of sinful
man to be a sin offering. And so he condemned sin in sinful man, in
order that the righteous requirements of the law might be fully met in
us, who do not live according to the sinful nature but according to the
Spirit.

That the righteousness of the law might be fulfilled where? In us,
provided, of course, that we walk how? Not after the flesh but after
the Spirit.

So please remember that the victory of Christ is ours. Now
all these wonderful victories, overcoming, can be summed up in
one passage, and that is specially applying to the last generation
of Christians, and that is Revelation 15. When, finally, Laodicea
repents, turns from self-dependence to God-dependence, and walks
by faith alone, this is what is going to happen. This is the ultimate
goal of the Laodicean message for God's people, and that's found in

Revelation 15:2-4:

And I saw what looked like a sea of glass mixed with fire and, standing beside the sea, those who had been victorious over the beast and his image and over the number of his name. They held harps given them by God and sang the song of Moses the servant of God and the song of the Lamb: "Great and marvelous are your deeds, Lord God Almighty. Just and true are your ways, King of the ages. Who will not fear you, O Lord, and bring glory to your name? For you alone are holy. All nations will come and worship before you, for your righteous acts have been revealed."

Standing beside the sea of glass mixed with fire were those who had been victorious over:

1. The beast,
2. His image, and
3. The number of his name.

So this is God's purpose for Laodicea. Now the question is, "What is the secret of this victory? How can we attain it?" Well, I gave you a clue, but let me give you a couple of texts that will help you. Turn to 1 John 4 and I want you to look at verse 4. This is one of the great promises of the Bible, this is one of the greatest truths of righteousness by faith. Now I want you to get the context. The context is overcoming the false prophets and the antichrist, which we know is the beast, and those that deceive. Okay, look at verse 3:

...But every spirit that does not acknowledge Jesus is not from God. This is the spirit of the antichrist, which you have heard is coming and even now is already in the world.

But now look at verse 4:

You, dear children, are from God and have overcome them [i.e., these false prophets, the antichrist, the beast, and his mark and his image and all], *because* [how have we overcome?] *the one who is in you is greater than the one who is in the world.*

There are two people here. "The one who is in you is greater than the one who is in the world." Who is the "he" that is in the world? Satan. And Who is the "He" that is in you? Christ in you, the hope of glory.

Now please remember, if you go to Romans 8:2, Paul tells us that:

...Because through Christ Jesus the law of the Spirit of life set me free from the law of sin and death.

Okay, now Christ dwells in you and me through the Holy Spirit. And so the Holy Spirit, Who represents Christ dwelling in you, is greater than he that is in the world. Okay, I want to give you a similar idea, this time through the writings of Paul. 2 Corinthians 10:4-5. Now I want you to notice what Paul is saying here:

The weapons we fight with are not the weapons of the world. On the contrary, they have divine power to demolish strongholds. We demolish arguments and every pretension that sets itself up against the knowledge of God, and we take captive every thought to make it obedient to Christ.

I want to explain verse 3, because verse 3 can be confusing:

For though we live in the world, we do not wage war as the world does.

What does he mean, "though we live in the world" ("though we walk in the flesh," in some translations)? Well, he means the same thing here as he did in Galatians 2:20:

I have been crucified with Christ and I no longer live, but Christ lives in me. The life I live in the body, I live by faith in the Son of God, who loved me and gave himself for me.

So what he means in verse 3 is, even though we still have this flesh, even though we are still in this world with this human nature of ours, this sinful human nature, we do not use this flesh to conquer sin. "We do not wage war as the world does" means we do not use this natural power of ours to overcome sin because we can't do it. Or to produce righteousness. We can't do it, we saw it.

The weapons we fight with are not the weapons of the world. On the contrary, they have divine power to demolish strongholds. [Please notice what you can do with Christ in you.] We demolish arguments and every pretension that sets itself up against the knowledge of God, and we take captive every thought to make it obedient to Christ.

It's only through the power of God that we can overcome self.

Is it possible for a believer to bring every thought under control by the indwelling Christ? The Bible says yes. Now please remember, this is the joys, the fruits of the gospel. This is not what saves you. This is the evidence of the power of the gospel in you. So please don't get the idea that you have to do this in order to be saved. No, you have to do this in order for you to overcome, and sit on the throne of God, and to reflect His glory.

Okay, now comes the big question: "What is the cost for Christ to dwell in you?" Because this is something that we must face. What is the cost? And I can sum up the cost in one word: "brokenness." But let me give you a couple of texts and then I'll give you an illustration. Please turn to John 12. There is a cost, folks. Let me put it this way as we turn to this passage: when Christ lives in you, and produces His righteousness in you — what we call imparted righteousness — who gets the glory, God or you? God. How does the flesh feel about it? It gets hurt.

Here is what Jesus is saying, John 12:24:

I tell you the truth, unless a kernel of wheat falls to the ground and dies, it remains only a single seed. But if it dies, it produces many seeds.

Jesus is using the grain as a symbol. The shell of the wheat is pretty hard. The life is not in the shell; it is inside, in the germ. This shell has to be broken by the work of water. It has to be softened and broken so that life may spring out of that and produce fruit.

I'll give you another statement with the same example. 1 Corinthians 15, except Paul is using much stronger words than Jesus Christ but he's saying the same thing. 1 Corinthians 15:36. He's using this as an illustration of the power of the resurrection, too.

How foolish! What you sow does not come to life unless it dies.

When you plant a grain of wheat into the ground, it does not come to life until that outer shell dies, or is broken, or disintegrates. Now I'm going to give you another text and then we'll go to the example. Now turn to 2 Corinthians 4 and I want you to notice the statement that Paul makes in verse 7:

But we have this treasure in jars of clay to show that this all-surpassing power is from God and not from us.

We are the shell, folks; we are the earthen vessel, the jar of clay. Where does God dwell, in the outward man or in the inward man? Paul will use these phrases: "the inner man" and "the outer man." Okay, now here's the problem, and I'll give the illustration. The illustration is found in Matthew 26:6, 7:

While Jesus was in Bethany in the home of a man known as Simon the Leper, a woman came to him with an alabaster jar of very expensive perfume, which she poured on his head as he was reclining at the table.

There are other passages in the gospel. The illustration is about Mary. She comes to Jesus and she has a box with her. What is the box made of? Alabaster. Have you seen alabaster? It's quite a pretty stone. When you buy an expensive ointment, or when you buy expensive perfume, it comes in very beautiful bottles, the bottles are very pretty, aren't they? So that after you use the perfume you keep it because the bottles are very pretty. Okay, now the alabaster box had inside a very expensive or very precious ointment called spikenard. And the bottle or the box was sealed. When Mary brought the box, nobody knew what was inside the box until she broke it. Then the whole room was filled with the smell of this precious ointment.

Now, Colossians 1:27 says that Christ is dwelling in every believer:

To them God has chosen to make known among the Gentiles the glorious riches of this mystery, which is Christ in you, the hope of glory.

Remember, "you in Christ" is your ticket to heaven. "Christ in you" is the "hope of glory." Now, the trouble is, nobody can see Christ in you until the outer shell is broken. When Mary broke that bottle, it was only then that everybody in the room could smell the fragrance.

But here's the problem. We are great admirers of the alabaster box, which is our outward self. We think that the church cannot do without us. Some of us feel that, without our degrees, the church would never exist. Some of us feel that, without our administrative abilities, the church would collapse. Some of us feel that "without me" this church would never exist. Folks, I want to give you some bad news: you are not indispensable. The church can survive without you. It cannot survive without Christ. So please don't ever get the idea, when God uses you mightily, that the church cannot do without you. It is Christ in you that is the hope of glory.

And for that inner Christ to shine outwardly, something has to take place. This shell, this clay jar, must be broken. We are vase admirers, folks, but the world needs to see not how good we are, which is self-righteousness, but how good Christ is. And that will only take place when this earthen vessel, this clay jar, is broken. Now with this in mind, I want you sometime on your own to read this whole passage of 2 Corinthians 4. But I want you to look at verse 16 and 17 where Paul makes a conclusion:

Therefore we do not lose heart. Though outwardly we are wasting away, yet inwardly we are being renewed day by day. For our light and momentary troubles are achieving for us an eternal glory that far outweighs them all.

So our outward man should perish. Now let me give you some more texts in this passage. Look at verse 10:

We always carry around in our body the death of Jesus, so that the life of Jesus may also be revealed in our body.

Please notice, we must die with Christ. For Christ's life to shine out of you, you must die with Christ. Verse 11:

For we who are alive are always being given over to death for Jesus' sake, so that his life may be revealed in our mortal body.

So Christian living, or overcoming, involves two processes that take place simultaneously: on the one hand, I must die so that, on the other hand, Christ must live. In other words, "not I, but Christ." And I'll tell you, folks, the hardest part, especially in the realm of self-righteousness is, "not I." It's the hardest part. And that's what I want to remind you of what Jesus said in John 15, at the end of verse 5:

I am the vine; you are the branches. If a man remains in me and I in him, he will bear much fruit; apart from me you can do nothing.

"Without Me you can do nothing."

And He's talking here in the context of fruit-bearing. With this in mind, I want to conclude with two verses. First I want to go to the Lord Jesus Christ, Luke 9:23. He's talking here to the disciples, which means that He's talking to us today:

Then he said to them all: "If anyone would come after me, he must deny himself and take up his cross daily and follow me."

Now, it is easy to say deny self in terms of sin, but, folks, in the Laodicean context, we need to deny self-righteousness. It's very painful to our ego. Let us learn from the Apostle Paul, this is why I want to conclude with Paul, Philippians 2. And as we turn to this passage, let me ask you a question: "What was the greatest struggle, as you read your four gospels, what was the greatest struggle that Jesus had throughout His life?" You will notice that it is over the problem of self. Let me give you just one example, His final battle at Gethsemane (Luke 22:42):

"Father, if you are willing, take this cup from me; yet not my will [or self-will], *but yours be done."*

And Jesus denied self to the very end. Philippians 2:5 (and you can connect this with Romans 12):

Your attitude should be the same as that of Christ Jesus....

Now what kind of mind or attitude did Christ have? Verses 6-8 explain the mind of Christ:

...Who, being in very nature God, did not consider equality with God something to be grasped, but made himself nothing, taking the very nature of a servant, being made in human likeness. And being found in appearance as a man, he humbled himself and became obedient to death — even death on a cross!

It was a mind of self-emptying. He was equal with God, He did not cling to His equality, but He let go. And He went down and down and He became obedient unto death, even the death of the cross. He never allowed self to dominate Him. And Paul's plea is, "Let this mind be in you which was in Christ Jesus."

What is the Laodicean messages' ultimate goal? God wants a people, not just individuals, but He wants a people, through whom

He wants to lighten the earth with His glory. And that's Revelation 18:1, the fourth angel:

After this I saw another angel coming down from heaven. He had great authority, and the earth was illuminated by his splendor.

When that happens, folks, there will be no excuse for anyone to be lost, because God will demonstrate the power of the gospel. And as Paul said in 1 Corinthians 4:20:

For the kingdom of God is not a matter of talk but of power.

And God wants to demonstrate this, and He will say to the universe, He will say to the world, the disbelieving world, "Here are my people. They have the faith of Jesus. And they have overcome."

And the devil will say, "Okay, let me test them." And folks, they will be tested. How bad will be the test? It will be a test that no other generation has ever experienced. We will look at the test towards the end of our studies. When the test comes, will the Laodicean church overcome? Well, God has promised in His Bible that there will be a people who overcome. The question is, "Are you willing to be broken? Are you willing to say, 'Not I,' that the second half of that formula may be realized in your life?"

Now the issue is not whether you're going to heaven or not. The issue is that the world desperately needs to see Christ in you, the hope of glory. Laodicea must overcome. The stumbling block to her overcoming is the problem of self. It is not so much that she's doing terribly bad things, her problem is self-righteousness. And so the world is waiting, folks, the world is waiting to see God, not to see man, but God manifested in the flesh.

And Jesus says to us, as He said to the disciples 2,000 years ago, "You are the light of the world. Let this light shine." But, unfortunately, we have the light, but it is under a bushel, which is our humanity, the greatest hindrance. And I pray to God that this humanity will be willing to be surrendered to the cross.

When you look at the fruits of the Spirit in Galatians 5:22-25, you will notice that Paul says that those who are belonging to Christ have crucified the flesh:

But the fruit of the Spirit is love, joy, peace, patience, kindness, goodness, faithfulness, gentleness and self-control. Against such things there is no law. Those who belong to Christ Jesus have crucified the sinful nature with its passions and desires. Since we live by the Spirit, let us keep in step with the Spirit.

The Holy Spirit cannot shine out of you unless you open the door and let Him take over. And that is what we covered last study. So my prayer, folks, is that we would be willing to become *nothing* that He may be everything in us. That is not very easy for the flesh. It means that when people don't appreciate you, you'll be willing to be hurt. It means that when you are not appreciated, you will be willing to go on. And that's hard.

You know, our pioneers in the mission field had to face lions, and hardships, physical hardships. Today, the greatest issue that you face in the mission field is ingratitude. Because, you see, the Third World does not like missionaries, because the word "missionary" implies they are still backwards.

I will never forget my first experience as a colporteur, as a literature evangelist in England. I made the greatest mistake when I knocked on the door. I told them that I was from Africa, and one lady opened my eyes. She said, "Look, it is we English people who sent missionaries to Africa. It is not the other way around." In other words, "You need missionaries, we don't. We are a Christian country."

Well, today, the Third World feels the same: "We don't need you. Go home." And that is why, folks, many, many missionaries, I would say even the majority, do not fulfill their entire term. They sign a contract for six years; most of them come back home before the six years are up. Why? One of the main reasons is because the people don't appreciate you. Not so much our own members, but the people in the country, the officials, the government officials. They'll say, "Go home, we don't need you. We can preach here without you."

Are you willing to swallow your pride? Are you willing to be hurt by another church member and not give up, and say, "I will push on." Are you familiar with that statement of Ellen G. White where she says in the last days we have to take courage from, "Draw warmth from the coldness of others." That's the condition that we have to reach. So when somebody says something hard, and that hurts your pride, please don't give up the church and say, "I will stop coming to church, the pastor said so and so to me."

When Jesus came to this world, was He appreciated? No. John 1:11:

He came to that which was his own, but his own did not receive him.

What would happen to you and to me if Christ said, "Look, these people don't appreciate me, I'll go back"? What would happen to us? Christ did not care what they did with Him. They spat on Him. Are you willing to be loyal to Christ even though you're insulted or mocked at and spat at? The world spat on Jesus Christ, they did not appreciate Him, they accused Him falsely, and yet He overcame. He overcame pride, He overcame self. He was willing to be nothing that you and I might be in His kingdom.

That was the attitude of John the Baptist. John the Baptist was willing to be nothing. John 3:30:

"He must become greater; I must become less."

If any of you go to the mission field, please have this attitude: the national must increase and the missionary must decrease in position. Because that's the only way to finish the work. We're having endless problems because for years the missionaries did not want to decrease and now the nationals want to increase, which is the wrong attitude.

Folks, this will not finish the work. The work will be finished when God has a people who surrendered self to the cross and let the Holy Spirit take over. Then the earth will be lightened with His glory, but we must begin in our own churches, in our own towns. We must lighten the earth with His glory, how do we do it? Not by trying, folks. "This is our victory, even our faith." And faith means, "Not I, but Christ." And this is my prayer for each one of you.

CHAPTER ELEVEN

LAODICEA IS SEALED

Revelation 7:1-8:

After this I saw four angels standing at the four corners of the earth, holding back the four winds of the earth to prevent any wind from blowing on the land or on the sea or on any tree. Then I saw another angel coming up from the east, having the seal of the living God. He called out in a loud voice to the four angels who had been given power to harm the land and the sea: "Do not harm the land or the sea or the trees until we put a seal on the foreheads of the servants of our God." Then I heard the number of those who were sealed: 144,000 from all the tribes of Israel. From the tribe of Judah 12,000 were sealed, from the tribe of Reuben 12,000, from the tribe of Gad 12,000, from the tribe of Asher 12,000, from the tribe of Naphtali 12,000, from the tribe of Manasseh 12,000, from the tribe of Simeon 12,000, from the tribe of Levi 12,000, from the tribe of Issachar 12,000, from the tribe of Zebulun 12,000, from the tribe of Joseph 12,000, from the tribe of Benjamin 12,000.

Please turn your Bibles, this time, to Revelation 7. We're going to deal this study and next study on the 144,000. Many have been looking forward to this, to see what kind of solution this bush preacher will come up with. It's been a subject that has caused much controversy in our history.

I want to first of all link this message and our next study to our study of the Laodicean message. I want to remind you of our last study, that, unlike the other six churches, Christ does not only want Laodicea to overcome, but He wants her to overcome "even as He overcame."

Now since we follow the Historicist approach to the book of Revelation and Daniel, then the Laodicean people represent the last generation of Christians. As such, they will face the final showdown in the great controversy between Christ and Satan. There has to be a final showdown. The book of Revelation defines this final showdown as the war of Armageddon.

That is another subject that is very confusing. We won't have time to go into the war of Armageddon but I would like to just look at it. Turn to Revelation 16. I would like to recommend a book to you; it's called *Chariots of Salvation, the Biblical Drama of Armageddon*. It's the finest book on the subject that I've ever read. Even Evangelical scholars are admitting that this is one of the finest interpretations on the war of Armageddon. In fact, Longman, who's a professor at the Westminster Theological Seminary, says that "This is a much needed corrective to the popular views of the end time as regards the war of Armageddon."

But I want you to notice something which he brings out in very clear detail concerning what the book of Revelation has to say about the war Armageddon. Reading from Revelation 16:13-16. Verse 13:

Then I saw three evil spirits that looked like frogs; they came out of the mouth of the dragon, out of the mouth of the beast and out of the mouth of the false prophet.

These three unclean spirits are, you might say, the opposite of the Three Angels' Message. The Three Angels' Message brings God's message and prepares a people for the end time. Here the three unclean spirits prepare the world for the time of trouble, for this great showdown, this final conflict between Christ and Satan. And, of course, these are false prophets. Now look at verse 14:

They are spirits of demons performing miraculous signs, and they go out to the kings of the whole world, to gather them for the battle on the great day of God Almighty.

Please notice, it is "the battle of that great day of God Almighty." It is not a Middle East crisis, it has nothing to do with the Middle East. It is the final showdown between God and Satan, and of course, between God's people and Satan's people, the world. And God will prepare His people through the three angels' message; Satan is preparing his people through the three unclean Spirits. And look now at the next verse, verse 15. Please notice, this will take place just prior to the second coming of Christ.

"Behold, I come like a thief! Blessed is he who stays awake and keeps his clothes with him, so that he may not go naked and be shamefully exposed."

Now please link this with the Laodicean message. What did Jesus offer Laodicea in Revelation 3:18?

I counsel you to buy from me ... white clothes to wear, so you can cover your shameful nakedness....

And here in Revelation 16 we are to "keep" that garment, hold on to the righteousness of Christ by faith up to the very end. And, of course, verse 16 says:

Then they gathered the kings together to the place that in Hebrew is called Armageddon.

That's where the word, "Armageddon" comes from. This is the final showdown. Okay now, this battle, when we look at it from the Christian point of view, is known as the "Great Tribulation," where God's people will be tried in a way that has never been experienced by any generation in the past. I would like to look at two passages in the Old Testament that describe this great tribulation. One is in Daniel 12:1:

At that time [i.e., when the ministry of Christ is finished in heaven] *Michael, the great prince who protects your people, will arise. There will be a time of distress such as has not happened from the beginning of nations until then. But at that time your people — everyone whose name is found written in the book* [i.e., the book of life] *— will be delivered.*

In other words, those who hold on, those who endure unto the end, God will deliver them. Okay, turn backwards to Jeremiah 30:7 which says basically the same thing as Daniel 12:1. Both prophets tell us that it's the time of trouble that has never been experienced by any previous generation.

How awful that day will be! None will be like it. It will be a time of trouble for Jacob, but he will be saved out of it.

Please notice, Jacob's trouble was a wrestling. And remember, even though Jacob was injured — his hip was very painfully dislocated — he held on, he held on to the angel and said, "I will not let you go until you bless me."

With this in mind, the question is, "What will be the real issue in the time of trouble? What is it that we have to overcome?" I believe, folks, that in this great tribulation, the victory of the cross must be reproduced, the victory of the cross of Jesus Christ must be reproduced. Now what do I mean by the victory of the cross? In Luke 23:35-39, three times — once through the soldiers, once through the priests, and once through the thief on the left hand side — three times the devil tempted Jesus Christ to come down from the cross and save Himself. Now, could He do it? The answer is yes; He was God. He could come down, independent of the Father, and save Himself. Did He come down? No. Well, I want you to listen to how Ellen G. White describes those last moments as He hung on the cross and He faced this terrible temptation. You need to read the whole chapter, it's the chapter on Calvary, but I want to read the conclusion of this chapter, page 756, of *Desire of Ages*:

Amid the awful darkness, apparently forsaken of God, Christ had drained the last dregs in the cup of human woe. [This was the final test.] In those dreadful hours he had relied upon the evidence of His Father's acceptance hitherto given Him. He was acquainted with the character of His Father. He understood His justice, [but He had to go through this] His mercy and His great love. By faith [please notice, not by feeling, but by faith] He rested in Him Whom it had ever been His joy to obey. And as in submission He submitted Himself to God, the sense of the loss of His Father's favour was withdrawn.... By faith Christ was victor. [It is by faith He overcame.]

His feelings told Him that God had forsaken Him. His faith told Him that God will not forsake Him. By faith, He was victorious. And in the time of trouble, folks, our faith will be tested to its bitter end. Of course, those whose faith will endure the great tribulation are called in the Bible the 144,000. These represent Laodicea who has overcome, even as Christ has overcome.

Now I want to give you another text that reveals the issue in the great tribulation. I've given you two that simply tell you that there will be a time of trouble that has never been experienced by any previous generation. But turn to Isaiah 54 and notice how Isaiah describes this terrible event. I'll read verse 5-7, you may want to read the whole chapter. The subtitle in my Bible says, "The church comforted with gracious promises." And that is true.

"For your Maker [we know this refers to Christ, He's the Creator] *is your husband — the Lord Almighty is his name — the Holy One of Israel is your Redeemer; he is called the God of all the earth. The Lord will call you back as if you were a wife deserted and distressed in spirit — a wife who married young, only to be rejected," says your God. "For a brief moment I abandoned you, but with deep compassion I will bring you back."*

So for a small moment God will forsake us, or if I may use the words of Ellen G. White, "We will feel apparently forsaken of God" during the great tribulation. In the final showdown, God will say, "Here are My people who have the faith of Jesus Christ." And the devil will say, "Okay, give them into my hands." And God will say, "Okay, you can touch them, you can do anything you like with them, but you cannot kill them."

And we will be, folks, at the mercy of the world which is now controlled by the devil. And Jesus, while looking at this while He was on this earth, looking ahead, He made this statement in Luke 18. In Luke 18 Jesus tells us a parable, I want you to notice why He told this parable. Because verse 1 of chapter 18 tells us why. We will not go into the parable itself, you can read it at home, it's the parable of the unjust judge. But listen to the introduction, Luke 18:1:

Then Jesus told his disciples a parable to show them that they should always pray and not give up.

I want you to notice His conclusion about this parable, verse 8:

I tell you, he will see that they get justice, and quickly. [Notice He's talking about the unjust judge, but now He applies this to the last days.] *However, when the Son of Man comes* [that's the second coming of Christ], *will he find faith on the earth?*

Will there be a people whose faith will endure to the end? Well, I have good news, folks, the answer is yes. And the answer is found in Revelation 7. So now we can turn to Revelation 7. There are only two passages in the whole of the New Testament that discuss the 144,000. One is chapter 7 which we'll do in this study and the other is chapter 14. One is in the context of the sixth seal, the other one is in the context of the Three Angels' Message. And today we will deal with chapter 7, and I want you to look at it purely Biblically; forget your preconceived ideas. We will look at this Biblically. Now chapter 7 of Revelation is answering a question. The question is found in Revelation 6:17:

For the great day of their wrath has come...

Four times Paul says that the "wrath of God" is revealed from heaven when God withdraws, He gives them up. In that context, He has given them up to their own views but here is when God will withdraw His protection from God's people and at the second coming of Christ He will withdraw His protection from the unbelievers. But now look at Revelation 6:17:

For the great day of their wrath has come, and who can stand?

Now to understand that question we need to look at the context. Revelation 6 is dealing with the six seals. So we are looking at this chapter in the context of the seals. Now if you read chapter 6 you will notice that John spends an average of two verses for each seal. Seal number one is Revelation 6:1 and 2. Seal number 2 is verses 3 and 4, seal number 3 is 5 and 6, seal number 4 is 7 and 8, and seal number 5 is 9, 10, and 11. And seal number 6 begins with Revelation 6:12 and where does it end? With Revelation 7:17. Because Revelation 8:1 is the seventh seal.

So you notice that he is spending much of his time on the sixth seal. Now what is the sixth seal about? What's the context of the sixth seal? Well very clearly, it is the second coming of Christ and events preceding that. Look at Revelation 6:12-14:

I watched as he opened the sixth seal. There was a great earthquake. The sun turned black like sackcloth made of goat hair, the whole moon turned blood red, and the stars in the sky fell to earth, as late figs drop from a fig tree when shaken by a strong wind. The sky receded like a scroll, rolling up, and every mountain and island was removed from its place.

Now look at verse 15 and 16; here are the events preceding the second coming of Christ, and the second coming of Christ itself. What do the unbelievers do at the second coming of Christ? Revelation 6:15-17:

Then the kings of the earth, the princes, the generals, the rich, the mighty, and every slave and every free man hid in caves and among the rocks of the mountains. They called to the mountains and the rocks, "Fall on us and hide us from the face of him who sits on the throne and from the wrath of the Lamb! For the great day of their wrath has come, and who can stand?"

Now if you look at verse 15, it seems to us that John is including everybody — the rich, the noble, the poor. Everybody will not be able to stand the second coming of Christ, which is, of course, bringing the war of Armageddon to a stop. I did not say to an end, but to a stop. I am convinced that the war of Armageddon will not end at the second coming of Christ. It will stop for a while. It will continue at the end of the millennium, when Satan's people will be raised. And it will end with the destruction of the wicked and the reinstating of the kingdom of God on this earth.

But in verse 17 John is asking the question, "Will there be anybody who will be able to stand this tremendous time of trouble and the second coming of Christ and the wrath of the Lamb?" In other words, Revelation 6:17 is a similar question that Jesus told in Luke 18:8b:

However, when the Son of Man comes, will he find faith on the earth?

Will God find a people whose faith has endured when He comes in the end? Will God produce a people who have reproduced the victory of the cross? Because the cross was a similar situation where God abandoned Christ and left Him in the hands of the world.

Okay, now look at Revelation 7:1. The answer to Revelation 6:17 is found in chapter 7, and the answer is, "Yes, God will have a people."

After this I saw four angels standing at the four corners of the earth, holding back the four winds of the earth to prevent any wind from blowing on the land or on the sea or on any tree.

Now, we know from Jeremiah 25:31-34 (and also 51:1-2) that winds symbolized war. Jeremiah 25:31-34:

"The tumult will resound to the ends of the earth, for the Lord will bring charges against the nations; he will bring judgment on all mankind and put the wicked to the sword," declares the Lord.

This is what the Lord Almighty says: "Look! Disaster is spreading from nation to nation; a mighty storm is rising from the ends of the earth."

At that time those slain by the Lord will be everywhere — from one end of the earth to the other. They will not be mourned or gathered up or buried, but will be like refuse lying on the ground.

Weep and wail, you shepherds; roll in the dust, you leaders of the flock. For your time to be slaughtered has come; you will fall and be shattered like fine pottery.

Jeremiah 51:1, 2:

This is what the Lord says: "See, I will stir up the spirit of a destroyer against Babylon and the people of Leb Kamai. I will send foreigners to Babylon to winnow her and to devastate her land; they will oppose her on every side in the day of her disaster.

Okay, remember, God says to Satan, "Here are my people," and Satan says, "Give them into my hands." And God says, "Not yet, until I will protect My people, I will hold the strife, the great tribulation, I will hold it until..." what? Revelation 7:2-4:

Then I saw another angel coming up from the east, having the seal of the living God. He called out in a loud voice to the four angels who had been given power to harm the land and the sea: "Do not harm the land or the sea or the trees until we put a seal on the foreheads of the servants of our God." Then I heard the number of those who were sealed: 144,000 from all the tribes of Israel.

The word "sealed," what does it mean? I want to give you an example of what it means. Turn to Romans 4. Remember, Paul taught that circumcision does not contribute at all towards our salvation. So one of the questions that the Jews were coming up with is, "If circumcision does not contribute towards salvation, why did God give it to Abraham, and through him to the Jews? Why?" And Paul tells us why, it was a seal. Look at Romans 4:11:

And he received the sign of circumcision, a seal of the righteousness that he had by faith while he was still uncircumcised....

When did he have righteousness by faith? Before he was circumcised. So please remember, circumcision did not give him righteousness by faith, it did something else; it sealed what he already had.

...So then, he is the father of all who believe but have not been circumcised, in order that righteousness might be credited to them.

In other words, circumcision did not give righteousness by faith, but it sealed something that he already had. In other words, it confirmed, or it authenticated, what he already had. Now, please keep this mind, because I believe, folks, in the last days, the seal will be the Sabbath. The Sabbath doesn't give us righteousness by faith, it only seals something that is already there. The meaning of circumcision and the meaning of Sabbath are synonymous. Circumcision simply means that we remove unbelief and totally rest in Christ. And if you want a good definition of circumcision, look at Philippians 3:3, where Paul says:

For it is we who are the circumcision, we who worship by the Spirit of God, who glory in Christ Jesus, and who put no confidence in the flesh....

What does "seal" mean? It means our faith becomes unshakeable, we have settled into the truth of Jesus Christ our righteousness, we have bought the white raiment from Christ and have made this our only hope, and we are no longer changeable. Because Abraham's faith fluctuated before the sealing. But now our faith is confirmed. If we are so settled in the truth, we have so clearly understood God, His character, His love, His mercy, that our faith now is completely resting in Him, then we are sealed. The Sabbath will only be a sign of that seal. If you want to look at the Sabbath as a sign of the seal, please look at Exodus 31, because the Sabbath was given as a sign. Exodus 31:13, and also verse 16:

Say to the Israelites, "You must observe my Sabbaths. This will be a sign between me and you [please notice, to Paul "sign" and "seal" are the same thing] *for the generations to come, so you may know that I am the Lord, who makes you holy."*

"The Israelites are to observe the Sabbath, celebrating it for the generations to come as a lasting covenant."

And by the way, Hebrews 10:14 tells us that by one sacrifice we were sanctified, we were made perfect:

...Because by one sacrifice he has made perfect forever those who are being made holy.

The Sabbath is only the sign, so please keep this in mind. So what does Revelation 7 say? God says, "Before I let go of my protection, My people must be sealed." Sealed where? In the forehead. Which to me means, they must have the mind of Christ. And if you want to know what the mind of Christ is, let me give you a couple of texts. Philippians 2:5:

Your attitude should be the same as that of Christ Jesus:...

What kind of mind or attitude? Philippians 2:6-8 explains the mind of Christ:

...Who, being in very nature God, did not consider equality with God something to be grasped, but made himself nothing, taking the very nature of a servant, being made in human likeness. And being found in appearance as a man, he humbled himself and became obedient to death — even death on a cross!

It was a mind that was totally emptied of self. But the other text is 1 Peter 4:1, which is a very interesting statement:

Therefore, since Christ suffered in his body, arm yourselves also with the same attitude, because he who has suffered in his body is done with sin.

(When you have the mind of Christ, by the way, your flesh, your human nature, will suffer.) When we have the mind of Christ, folks, we will cease from sin. Okay, now back to Revelation 7. God is going to seal His servants. Where is He going to seal them? In the forehead, which means that our minds will have been settled into the truth of Christ our righteousness. No more wavering. And it is in this context that Christ will say [Revelation 22:11]:

He that is unjust, let him be unjust still; and he which is filthy, let him be filthy still; and he that is righteous, let him be righteous still; and he that is holy, let him be holy still.

Why? Because he's sealed. Both camps have made up their mind. God's people have made up their mind, "This is where I will stand." And by the way, Jesus made up His mind in Gethsemane. You remember? He struggled in Gethsemane. It was in Gethsemane that He was sealed: "Not My will, but Thine." Matthew 26:39:

Going a little farther, he fell with his face to the ground and prayed, "My Father, if it is possible, may this cup be taken from me. Yet not as I will, but as you will."

And He carried out the effects of that sealing.

Abraham was sealed at circumcision. Seventeen years later he was tested. We will be sealed before the time of great tribulation. Now comes the big question, "How many are sealed?" The answer is, "The 144,000." Is this literal or is this figurative? Well, I can only give you my position. Look at Revelation 7:4. I want you to notice that John does not see how many are sealed, he only heard. Keep that in mind.

Then I heard the number of those who were sealed: 144,000 from all the tribes of Israel.

There are two ways that we can interpret the word, "Israel." If we insist that the 144,000 are literal, then "Israel" must also be literal. Which means that there's no hope for us, folks; it's only Jews. If 144,000 is symbolic, then Israel must also be symbolic. Symbolic of what? Well, keep your finger here, and I'll tell you how the New Testament interprets the symbol of Israel. Romans 9:6-8. Let me quickly give you the context.

God had promised Abraham, God had promised Israel, that ALL the seed of Abraham will be saved. Okay? ALL, no exception. All the seed of Abraham will be saved. That was a promise made by God. Now comes the Apostles telling the Jews that you are lost. And the Jews retorted, "Okay, if we are lost, then God has failed to keep His promise." And Paul says, "No, God will keep His promise." And this is what he says in Romans 9:6-8:

It is not as though God's word had failed. ["God will keep His promise, but the problem is your interpretation of 'Israel.'"] *For not all who are descended from Israel are Israel.* [So God doesn't consider all Jews to be part of Israel. Then who is Israel?] *Nor because they are his descendants are they all Abraham's children. On the contrary, "It is through Isaac that your offspring will be reckoned." In other words, it is not the natural children who are God's children, but it is the children of the promise who are regarded as Abraham's offspring.*

God gave Israel three fathers: Abraham, Isaac, and Jacob. If you look at those three fathers, they represent the qualities of God's people. Abraham stands for faith, which Romans 4 brings out. Isaac stands for the new birth, "born from above." And remember what Jesus said to Nicodemus? John 3:3,5:

In reply Jesus declared, "I tell you the truth, no one can see the kingdom of God unless he is born again."

Jesus answered, "I tell you the truth, no one can enter the kingdom of God unless he is born of water and the Spirit."

Unless you're born from above, you can't enter the kingdom of God. In other words, you can't belong to Israel, unless you're a child, symbolic of Israel, of Isaac. Not blood child, but symbolic child. And, of course, Jacob represents those who endure unto the end. And that's why the time of trouble, the great tribulation is called, "the time of Jacob's trouble" because he endured.

What Paul is saying here is that Israel is those who do not have the blood of Abraham, or the blood of Isaac, but those who are, like Isaac, born from above. Look at Romans 9:8:

In other words, it is not the natural children who are God's children, but it is the children of the promise who are regarded as Abraham's offspring.

And who are the children of the promise? Those who have the faith in Christ and who are born again, and have put on Christ, they are Abraham's seed and heirs according to the promise. Galatians 3:27-29:

...For all of you who were baptized into Christ have clothed yourselves with Christ. There is neither Jew nor Greek, slave nor free, male nor female, for you are all one in Christ Jesus. If you belong to Christ, then you are Abraham's seed, and heirs according to the promise.

I believe that the 144,000 are symbolic, and that the word "Israel" does not refer to the Jews, but to the Christians, Jews and Gentiles, who have the experience of the 12 tribes, because each tribe stands for an experience. Therefore, to me, the 144,000 are symbolic. But that's not the only answer I have for you, I want to go further.

God seals them, but please remember the context. Before God removes His protection and allows Satan to initiate the great war of Armageddon, God's people are sealed. How many are sealed? 12,000 from each tribe, which makes, of course, 12 times 12,000 is 144,000. I want to say something here that you may not be aware of: some of the manuscripts (not all, but quite a few of the reliable manuscripts) when it comes to this verse 4, and the others also, they do not write, "144,000" like you see in your Bible, in words. The 144 is in words and the thousand is in numbers.

So we have 144, and then one, zero, zero, zero; three zeros, that's a 1,000. It's a very strange way of writing, which means that John was kind of making a distinction between 144 and thousand. And I have wrestled with this. I can only give you an opinion. It may not be right. The 144 represents the church, 12 from each tribe, 12 times 12 is 144. The thousand to me represents the Most Holy Place, because the dimensions of the Most Holy Place were 10 cubits by 10 cubits by 10 cubits, and so the space, the volume of that space was 1,000, and a thousand represents the ministry of Christ in the Most Holy Place where He will prepare people who will able to stand. Now that's only my opinion for what it's worth. But now let's go back to Revelation 7. Look at verse 9:

After this I looked and there before me was a great multitude that no one could count, from every nation, tribe, people and language, standing before the throne and in front of the Lamb. They were wearing white robes and were holding palm branches in their hands.

I'll tell you why I believe John doesn't see the people who are sealed but hears the number. I think it's because the 144,000 were not in one place, they were scattered over the world. They are not located in one place, they are scattered. They are not in the Middle East, they are all over the world, therefore he can't see them in one place. But after they have gone through the great tribulation, and after they have withstood the second coming of Christ, now John doesn't hear but he sees:

After this I looked and there before me was a great multitude that no one could count, from every nation, tribe, people and language, standing before the throne and in front of the Lamb. They were wearing white robes and were holding palm branches in their hands.

Now many feel that verse 9 refers to the great multitude that were saved. Others say that this is the great multitude that the 144,000 converted. Well, we have no Biblical evidence for these interpretations. I believe verse 9 is referring to the 144,000, and I'll give you my reasons:

1. The context of Revelation 7 is only the 144,000. Those who will be able to stand. That's argument number one.
2. The second argument is that these people were clothed with white robes and palms in their hands and when I turn to Revelation 19:7-8, I discover that the white robes is the imparted righteousness of Christ, which this last generation of Christians will experience:

"Let us rejoice and be glad and give him glory! For the wedding of the Lamb has come, and his bride has made herself ready. Fine linen, bright and clean, was given her to wear." (Fine linen stands for the

righteous acts of the saints.)

1. But my third argument is a very powerful one, and that is in verse 13. One of the elders — remember that there are 24 elders, and these elders are human beings saved — so here is one of the elders (who represent all of the saved) who asks a question, and the question is in connection with verse 9. Look at verse 13:

Then one of the elders asked me, "These in white robes — who are they, and where did they come from?"

So to whom is the elder referring? To verse 9, the great multitude which were dressed in white robes. "Who are these special people, and where did they come from?" Now please remember, it could not, therefore, refer to all the saved because the elders belong to all the saved. But now look at the answer [Revelation 7:14-17]:

I answered, "Sir, you know."

And he said, "These are they who have come out of the great tribulation [which you can't apply to the whole saved multitude]; *they have washed their robes and made them white in the blood of the Lamb.* [They have experienced the total victory, they have overcome as Christ overcame.] *Therefore, they are before the throne of God and serve him day and night in his temple* [which will be a privilege only for the 144,000]; *and he who sits on the throne will spread his tent over them. Never again will they hunger; never again will they thirst. The sun will not beat upon them, nor any scorching heat. For the Lamb at the center of the throne will be their shepherd; he will lead them to springs of living water. And God will wipe away every tear from their eyes."*

In other words, they will never ever go through that great tribulation again. They have been delivered out of it. So, folks, I believe that God will seal a great multitude of people. I believe that the gospel is the power of God.

Now I'll tell you, this was a big issue in our church, but you need to know the context of the issue. The reason why it was an issue in our church during the time of Ellen G. White was because our membership was approaching 144,000. And the members began to say, "What will happen when we reach 144,000?" Some of them were saying, "The end will come." We don't have that problem today because our membership is more than five million. The argument that it is literal came primarily because of our membership.

The other came from a statement which is not fair to use, because if you are going to find out what is the answer from Ellen G. White you can't just take one statement where she says, "I saw the 144,000..." and she says, "in number." And they say, "There! She says it's a number." But when Ellen G. White was asked personally, "Is it literal or is figurative?" She said, "Don't be bothered about this issue. Try and be among them."

So Sister White never gave a clear answer as to whether they were literal or whether they were figurative. And the reason for that was the church was being split over this issue — Is it figurative or is it literal? — because of our membership. And some of us are projecting this problem today. But the thing is this: chapter 7 of Revelation is answering the question, "Who will be able to stand?" Will God have a people whose faith can endure the great tribulation? And the answer is yes! Is it just a handful, a 144,000? No, it is a great multitude, but they have to be sealed first. They are a great multitude from every nation, kindred, tongue, and people. So they are scattered. But when Christ comes they will be joined together. They will be before His temple. They will be dressed in white raiment and they'll have palms, the victory sign. And God will give them a special privilege.

God wants to vindicate the power of the gospel. Are you willing to be one of those?

The great time of tribulation is terrible. I can't explain how terrible it is. All I can say is what Sister White says, that even our imagination cannot describe it. She says normally when we imagine problems, our imagination magnifies the problem. But in this case, no.

The only way I can describe the issue in the great time of tribulation is what Christ experienced on the cross. We will actually feel forsaken of God. We will feel forsaken of God. And the Devil will take advantage of those feelings. He will say, "You know why God has forsaken you? Because you are lost. He has abandoned you because there is no hope of salvation for you."

And your feelings will say there is no hope for you. But your faith will say, "I will never forsake you," that your righteousness is not in you, but in His son.

It will be the issue of righteousness by faith. Are you willing to rest in Christ, the Lord of the Sabbath, even though you feel forsaken, and you feel that you don't deserve heaven? And when, because your faith is sealed, you endure this great tribulation, and the devil will try and do his best, and he fails, then and then only will he pass the decree to kill them, which means that he is going beyond the bargain. And God will say, "No, you can't kill them." And that's when the earthquake will take place. And we who at that time will be hiding in the caves, will come out, and say, "This is the God that we have been waiting for. He has blessed us. We have endured the time of Jacob's trouble."

And those who have been hounding us will take our place in the caves, and they will say to the mountains and the rocks, "Fall on us. We can't bear the sight of this coming of Christ."

So God will have a people. And we, folks, we need to overcome. We need to overcome unbelief. We need to be circumcised, we need to remove all unbelief. We need to rest in Christ. We need to buy the white raiment, the righteousness of Christ. So stop looking at yourself for your assurance. Stop looking at your experience. Our part from beginning to end is faith. It is God's part to overcome sin. And faith is always a struggle, because by nature we are self-dependent.

May God bless us, that we may remain faithful. Our faith will become so strong that we will have the faith not only *in* Jesus Christ, but the faith *of* Jesus Christ. And that, of course, will be our next study.

CHAPTER TWELVE

LAODICEA IS FAULTLESS

Revelation 14:1-5:

Then I looked, and there before me was the Lamb, standing on Mount Zion, and with him 144,000 who had his name and his Father's name written on their foreheads. And I heard a sound from heaven like the roar of rushing waters and like a loud peal of thunder. The sound I heard was like that of harpists playing their harps. And they sang a new song before the throne and before the four living creatures and the elders. No one could learn the song except the 144,000 who had been redeemed from the earth. These are those who did not defile themselves with women, for they kept themselves pure. They follow the Lamb wherever he goes. They were purchased from among men and offered as firstfruits to God and the Lamb. No lie was found in their mouths; they are blameless.

The implication is that 144,000 is not just a literal number, but a vast multitude. There are two passages in the book of Revelation and two passages in the New Testament that deal with the 144,000. We touched the first passage in our last study, which is Revelation 7. This presents the 144,000 in the context of a question, and the question is, "Who will be able to stand the events preceding and leading up to the second coming of Christ?" And, as you know, the events preceding the second coming of Christ is the great tribulation, the war of Armageddon. And, of course, the coming of

Christ is also a tremendous event because Christ will not come with His glory veiled, but He will come in the full glory of His divinity.

Now I would like to turn to Revelation 14. You will notice here that the implication is the 144,000 are a vast multitude. Now, in Revelation 14 we are told the context of how the 144,000 will be produced. What will produce the 144,000? And the context of this section is the Three Angels' Message. It is the Three Angels' Message — which is righteousness by faith or Christ our righteousness — which will produce the 144,000.

The three angels' message can be described as the sealing message. It is a message that will prepare a people for the last days and the coming of Christ. It is also, as we shall see in our study, a message that is God's final call to a doomed world to accept His Son Jesus Christ. But I want now to look at the first five verses which describes the 144,000. Look at verse 1:

Then I looked...

Notice, John is not hearing, but he's doing what? He's looking. Remember we saw in Revelation 7, that when he heard, the people were scattered, but when he looked they were together in heaven. And you will notice that chapter 14 of Revelation is dealing with the 144,000 who have now arrived in heaven, and we shall see that by several statements here. Revelation 14:1:

Then I looked, and there before me was the Lamb, standing on Mount Zion [this is the coming of Christ], *and with him 144,000 who had his name and his Father's name written on their foreheads.*

The same concept is in chapter 7; this means that they have the mind of Christ. Now, in chapter 14, this name in their forehead, which is the seal of God, is contrasted with the mark of the beast. Look at verse 9. You will discover that there's a contrast here, the second half of Revelation 14:

...If anyone worships the beast and his image and receives his mark on the forehead or on the hand....

Please notice, there are two marks. One is the seal of God on the forehead, which is having the mind of Christ, and the other one is the mark of the beast. Okay, what this verse is saying, and what this passage is saying, is that when the Three Angels' Message is preached, it will divide the human race into only two camps. There will be nobody sitting on the fence, there will be only two camps: the believers and the unbelievers. As Christ mentioned once (Matthew 12:30):

He who is not with me is against me, and he who does not gather with me scatters.

There will be only two camps. Those who are for Christ will have surrendered themselves to the cross of Christ. They will say, "I am crucified with Christ. I am living, it is not I, but Christ."

The other ones will cry out, "Crucify Him!" Okay, so there's only two camps. Now the Bible describes these two groups in many ways: sheep and goats, the righteous and the wicked, those who build their house on the rock and those who build their house on the sand, the children of light and the children of darkness, and it goes on. You will find this dual description all through the New Testament. Now turn to verse 2, and please notice what John hears. He sees in verse 1 the 144,000 before the Lamb of God, now in verse 2 he hears. What does he hear?

And I heard a sound from heaven like the roar of rushing waters and like a loud peal of thunder. The sound I heard was like that of harpists playing their harps.

Now what does it mean, he hears rushing waters? In Africa, we have what we call flash floods. We have tremendous rains and the roads don't have bridges, because the country is poor, so they have what we call "dips," the dry river beds. When you travel those on a motorcycle, it's fun, because when you hit those dips and you come out you go up into the air. We had a pastor who was travelling, and he reached the bottom, and it was a bit wet, and his car got stuck, and as he was trying to push it out a flash flood came. It had rained in the mountains and it swept him and an African pastor and killed them both. It's like thunder, you hear it roaring along, and before you know it sweeps everything away.

This is the description here because you have the same concept in the Middle East. You have dry river beds. When it rains twice a year, the early rain and the latter rain, you have these flash floods. And John is saying, "I heard as if it was rushing water." In the book of Revelation, "water" represents people. Turn to Revelation 17:15, you will notice that the water is described here as people:

Then the angel said to me, "The waters you saw, where the prostitute sits, are peoples, multitudes, nations, and languages."

Please notice, waters represent a multitude of people. Now I want you to get the picture. He hears the voice as if it is of a rushing water. In other words, it is a numberless people. He hears the voices of uncountable people. It sounds like a great thunder, because that's what happens when you have these flash floods. You hear as if it's thunder and the next moment the water comes along. And what did he hear? It was (Revelation 14:2b):

The sound I heard was like that of harpists playing their harps.

To whom is verse 2 referring? Is it referring to all the saved? No, look at Revelation 14:3:

And they ["they" refers to verse 2, which refers to verse 1, the 144,000] *sang a new song before the throne* [so this has to be in heaven] *and before the four living creatures and the elders. No one could learn the song except the 144,000 who had been redeemed from the earth.*

"No one" means that none of the other saved could sing this song, except the 144,000. So this is in heaven, a vast multitude are singing this song, the 144,000 sing a new song before the throne, and before the four beasts.

Now there has been a problem with these four beasts. Who are these four beasts? There is much speculation. I am not sure myself, but I will tell you what I think. If you look at the description of the temple of God, you will notice that the temple was protected; even in the Most Holy Place the temple had the cherubims. If you look at the description of the cherubims in Ezekiel 10:14, you will find that these cherubims had faces, four different kinds of faces: ox, eagle, lion, and man. If you look at descriptions of the temple, you will notice that they have statues of the cherubim and each cherubim has a different face. Ezekiel 10:14:

Each of the cherubim had four faces: One face was that of a cherub [which is the Hebrew term for an ox], *the second the face of a man, the third the face of a lion, and the fourth the face of an eagle.*

By the way, all these four faces represent or symbolize the characteristics of Jesus Christ. The lion — He is the king. The eagle — He is victorious. The man — He is our Saviour. And the ox — He is our sacrifice. And remember, the cherubim was at the gate of Eden when our first parents were driven out, the cherubims were at the mercy seat. They represented Christ, our Saviour. So even through the angels, God revealed His saving grace.

The elders here represent the 24 elders who were redeemed as the first fruit. And, of course the "no one" refers to the rest of the saved. The elders couldn't sing it, the beasts couldn't sing it, no other person could sing it except the 144,000 who were redeemed from among mankind. Why is it that they could sing it? Well, verse 4 and verse 5 describes the spiritual qualities of these 144,000. Now we must not take these literally because this has caused problems. Look at verse 4:

These are those who did not defile themselves with women, for they kept themselves pure. They follow the Lamb wherever he goes. They were purchased from among men and offered as firstfruits to God and the Lamb.

If you take it literally, you would have to say that this is only men. What does it mean, "They did not defile themselves with women"? Turn to Revelation 17:5, because the context, you will notice in chapter 14, the context is between God's true people and God's enemies, which are identified with Babylon. And when we look at the Three Angels' Message, God is calling His people to come out of Babylon. Now look at Revelation 17:5:

This title was written on her forehead: MYSTERY, BABYLON THE GREAT, THE MOTHER OF PROSTITUTES AND OF THE ABOMINATIONS OF THE EARTH.

So these women here are the harlots, and the 144,000 were not defiled with their false teaching and their theology and all their human compromise. In other words, as we see when we look at the Three Angels' Message in other studies, you will discover that Babylon represents self. "Is this not great Babylon that who built? With whose power? For whose glory?" That is what Babylon stands for. But we'll come to that. Now the 144,000 had nothing to do with self. They had lost all confidence in the flesh and were rejoicing in whom?...in Christ.

In verse 4 it says, in some translations, "For they are virgins" ("they kept themselves pure"). I had one member come to me and say, "You know, no married person can be among the 144.000."

"Why?" I asked.

He said, "It says so. They have to be virgins."

Well, that's the problem with taking things literally. Please remember the book of Revelation is a symbolic book. What does John mean when he says, "they kept themselves pure"? I want to give you a text that will help you. Turn to 2 Corinthians 11:2 and, after looking at the verse, I want you to look at the context, because the context is very crucial, too. Listen to what Paul says to the Corinthians in 2 Corinthians 11:2:

I am jealous for you with a godly jealousy. I promised you to one husband, to Christ, so that I might present you as a pure virgin to him.

Now what's the context? Look at verse 3:

But I am afraid that just as Eve was deceived by the serpent's cunning, your minds may somehow be led astray from your sincere and pure devotion to Christ.

"I want you to be totally founded on Christ our righteousness. But I'm afraid that even though I have presented you as perfect in Christ, you are trying to turn away from it." Look at verse 4:

For if someone comes to you and preaches a Jesus other than the Jesus we [the apostles] *preached, or if you receive a different spirit from the one you received, or a different gospel from the one you accepted, you put up with it easily enough.*

And I want to remind you of John, "Don't believe every spirit. Any spirit who teaches that Christ has not come in the flesh is not of God; he's the antichrist."

For if someone comes to you and preaches a Jesus other than the Jesus we preached, or if you receive a different spirit from the one you received, or a different gospel from the one you accepted, you put up with it easily enough.

In other words, "I want to present you as a virgin to Christ, undefiled by philosophy, by human inventions and gimmicks. But I'm afraid that I can't do it because you're so easily swept from the gospel."

So please remember here, when he says in Revelation 14:4 that these are virgins, it means that they are no longer defiled by self or any human invention or philosophy. They are resting in Christ as their only hope, as their only Saviour. Is that clear? They're undefiled. That's what it means. They are virgins, they are undefiled. They are pure. And you remember what Jesus said in the sermon on the mount in Matthew 5? The very first thing He said, in verse 8:

Blessed are the pure in heart, for they will see God.

Okay, let's go on. "These are those who did not defile themselves with women," which means that they are resting entirely on Christ our righteousness. There's no self in it. "They kept themselves pure," which means that they are saying with Paul, "For me to live is Christ." Christ is everything to them. More in verse 4:

They follow the Lamb wherever he goes.

What does it mean, "to follow the Lamb"? The word "Lamb" is one of the terms used for Christ as a sacrifice. Remember, when John introduced Christ, what did he say? John 1:29:

The next day John saw Jesus coming toward him and said, "Look, the Lamb of God, who takes away the sin of the world!"

And the way that He does it is by the cross. What does it mean to "follow the Lamb wherever He goes"? Turn to Luke 9 and listen to what Jesus says Himself about following Him. And you will notice that it all agrees with the basic concept of righteousness by faith. It agrees, it is in harmony, with not being defiled with women, or being virgins. Luke 9:23:

Then he said to them all [His disciples]: *"If anyone would come after* [follow] *me, he must deny himself* [that is what the message of righteousness by faith demands] *and take up his cross daily and follow me."*

The cross is a symbol of the rejection of self. Let me put it another way, maybe I can give you a text, Galatians 5. What does the cross symbolize? Now please remember, to the Apostle Paul, the cross was not a piece of wood on which Christ died. The cross represented a truth. If you look at Luke 9:23, you will notice that Jesus said we must carry the cross or deny self how often? Daily. Did Christ carry the cross daily? Yes. Did He carry a piece of wood daily? No. Okay, so please, the cross in the New Testament, the emphasis is not the piece of wood. It is the truth. And I want to give you the truth. Galatians 5:24 and the context here is the fruits of the Spirit:

Those who belong to Christ Jesus have crucified the sinful nature with its passions and desires.

Now let me explain it to you in a very simple way. There are two things in each believer, there is "the flesh," which is our natural life. And there is "the Spirit," which is the Divine nature that we have become partakers of. And these two forces, these two things, the flesh and the Spirit, can never have partnership, they can never be married. The moment you try, you are defiling the truth, you're committing spiritual fornication. These two are enemies. That's why Paul says in Romans 8:7 that the carnal mind, the mind controlled by the flesh, is enmity with God and can never be subject to the law of God:

...The sinful mind is hostile to God. It does not submit to God's law, nor can it do so.

In Galatians 5:16-17, Paul makes it clear that the two are enemies:

So I say, live by the Spirit, and you will not gratify the desires of the sinful nature. For the sinful nature desires what is contrary to the Spirit, and the Spirit what is contrary to the sinful nature. They are in conflict with each other, so that you do not do what you want.

Now, because they are enemies, they are opposites. The flesh is founded on the principle of self. What the flesh sees, what the flesh desires, the flesh wants. At the very center of the flesh is covetousness. It covets everything. And we need to realize that this flesh will never be satisfied until it reaches the place of God. In other words, if God did not put restrictions to the flesh, where will the flesh end up? If you are getting in my way, my flesh will get rid of you, because you are in my way. How many people will the flesh get rid of to reach its ultimate goal? It has to get rid of even God, because the ultimate goal is to have the place of God.

By the way, the cross revealed that, and when you study it, you will discover that the cross reveals that if sin is given free reign, it will end up crucifying the son of God. That is why we cannot take sin lightly. Sin is more than simply doing something bad. Sin is taking the place of God. Sin is saying, "I, and not Christ." The gospel is saying, "Not I, but Christ." This is the difference between the Spirit and the flesh. The flesh says, "I", and the Spirit says, "Not I."

Now what happens when the Spirit says "no" to the flesh? Is the flesh happy? No, and I gave you a text in our last study, 1 Peter 4:1, when the Spirit says no to the flesh the flesh suffers. And here are God's people who are willing to suffer with Christ. All through His life, folks, from the time of His coming to this earth to the cross, Jesus stood on the platform of "not my will, but God's will be done." And all His life He suffered in the flesh, and God's will was performed. Now let's go on, back to the rest of Revelation 14:4:

They were purchased from among men and offered as firstfruits to God and the Lamb.

Now what does the word, "firstfruits" mean? It has more than one significance in the Bible. Let me give you two or three of them.

First, the word "firstfruits" means that the harvest time has approached. And you will notice, if you turn to Revelation 14:15, when the Three Angels Message has produced the 144,000, listen to what verse 15 says:

Then another angel came out of the temple and called in a loud voice to him who was sitting on the cloud [i.e., Jesus], "Take your sickle and reap, because the time to reap has come, for the harvest of the earth is ripe."

So the firstfruits is the sign that the harvest is ready, or around the corner.

The second is that the firstfruits symbolizes those that have reached maturity before the others. You see, the grain that has ripened first has rich maturity before the other grain which is still green. Or it can apply to fruit. In other words, even though the 144,000 are the last generations of Christians, they are the first ones to reach maturity in Christ. They are the firstfruits. Will all believers reach maturity? Yes, but where? In heaven. But the 144,000 will reach maturity here on earth. And, by the way, the Greek word for "maturity" in many of your Bibles is translated as the word, "perfect."

Now I want to give you one example of this maturity because it's in connection with the Three Angels' Message. Turn to Matthew 5, and I want you to notice what Jesus is describing here. In verse 43, He's describing the love that man can produce. This is the kind of love that we can generate. This is the kind of love that the Pharisees were teaching their people (Matthew 5:43):

You have heard that it was said, "Love your neighbor [which is your fellow men, or your fellow Jews, in that context] and hate your enemy."

Now in verses 44-48, Jesus says that this concept of love doesn't require you to be a Christian. Even the publicans can do that (Matthew 5:44-48):

But I tell you: Love your enemies and pray for those who persecute you, that you may be sons of your Father in heaven. He causes his sun to rise on the evil and the good, and sends rain on the righteous and the unrighteous. If you love those who love you, what reward will you get? Are not even the tax collectors doing that? And if you greet only your brothers, what are you doing more than others? Do not even pagans do that? Be perfect, therefore, as your heavenly Father is perfect.

What the gospel wants from you, what God wants from you, is to love others like God loves. And how does God love? Verse 44, does He love His enemies? Yes, Romans 5:10, "While we were enemies, we were reconciled to God by the death of His Son."

For if, when we were God's enemies, we were reconciled to him through the death of his Son, how much more, having been reconciled, shall we be saved through his life!

Luke 6:27-29:

But I tell you who hear me: Love your enemies, do good to those who hate you, bless those who curse you, pray for those who mistreat you. If someone strikes you on one cheek, turn to him the other also. If someone takes your cloak, do not stop him from taking your tunic.

Matthew 5:44:

But I tell you: Love your enemies and pray for those who persecute you....

Did the people curse Christ? Yes, and what did Christ say? "Forgive them." Did He do good to them that hated Him? Did He pray for them that persecuted Him, and despitefully used Him? Yes. And then is verse 45 (beginning with verse 44):

(But I tell you: Love your enemies and pray for those who persecute you,) that you may be sons of your Father in heaven.

And then He describes the love of the Father (verses 46-47):

He causes his sun to rise on the evil and the good, and sends rain on the righteous and the unrighteous. If you love those who love you [in other words, if you love just your neighbor], *what reward will you get? Are not even the tax collectors doing that? And if you greet only your brothers, what are you doing more than others? Do not even pagans do that?* [i.e., the unbelievers, the sinners do the same.]

And then when He finishes this in verse 48 He says:

Be perfect, therefore, as your heavenly Father is perfect.

What does He mean, "Be perfect (or mature)"? In other words, He says, "You must love without discrimination. You must love unconditionally, spontaneously, without the object of love being good to you. You must love others like God loves you." And this is the commandment that Jesus gave His disciples in John 13:34:

A new command I give you: Love one another. As I have loved you, so you must love one another.

Then in verse 35 He says:

By this all men will know that you are my disciples, if you love one another.

"By this shall ALL MEN know that you are my disciples, when you have this love, this agape love."

And folks, this is what the 144,000 will reflect. They will reflect the love of Jesus Christ. That is maturity. And it is in this sense that Jesus will say in Revelation 14:12:

This calls for patient endurance on the part of the saints who obey God's commandments and remain faithful to Jesus.

"Here are My people who are keeping the commandments."

Please, we must be clear about what Jesus means by keeping the commandments. Does He mean the letter, or does He mean the Spirit? The Jews were expert at the letter, and so are many Adventists. But it is the spirit that God is looking for. Okay, now remember that the "firstfruits" means:

1. They are the first ones to reach maturity.
2. They are the sign that the harvest is ripe.
3. They are the prototype of what others will be.

In other words, they are the ones who will manifest the full power of the gospel, while still on this earth. For example, turn to 1 Corinthians 15:23. Here Paul is using the firstfruits as a prototype. You see, some of the Corinthian believers were denying the resurrection of the believers. You will find that in verse 12. And Paul proves the resurrection of the believers not by the proof text method, but by the resurrection of Jesus Christ. The fact that Christ rose from the dead, guarantees whose resurrection? Ours. Now look at verse 23:

But each in his own turn: Christ, the firstfruits; then, when he comes, those who belong to him.

In other words, He's the prototype of our resurrection; because He rose, we will rise. He's the firstfruits. Our resurrection will take place at His coming.

Okay, will all the believers, will all the saved reflect the character of Christ? Yes. But not all have reached it will while they were on earth. The 144,000 will fully reflect the character of Christ. And this will be the greatest evidence of the power of the gospel, which is the power over sin and self. And then Revelation 14:5 simply describes this:

No lie was found in their mouths; they are blameless.

Some translations read, "And in their mouth was found no guile." Now there are two ways this word is used. For example, Psalms 32:2 speaks of having no guile in the spirit:

Blessed is the man whose sin the Lord does not count against him and in whose spirit is no deceit.

But in John 1:47, Jesus used the same word in an opposite sense: in terms of self-righteousness. If you read John 1:47, you will discover that Philip goes to his brother Nathanael, and do you know what he says to Nathanael? "I have found the Messiah!"

"Where did you find Him?" asks Nathanael.

"In Nazareth!"

Do you know what Nathanael replied? "Can anything good come out of Nazareth?" (No, it can't be. Nothing good can come out of Nazareth! He has the wrong lineage, the wrong birthplace.)

Well, Philip did not argue. He said, "Come and see."

And he came. And the first thing that Jesus said to Him was, "Here is an Israelite in whom there is no guile." (Who thinks he's very righteous; He doesn't come from Nazareth!) John 1:47:

When Jesus saw Nathanael approaching, he said of him, "Here is a true Israelite, in whom there is nothing false."

Nathaniel said to Jesus, "How do you know me?"

And Jesus said, "Well, when you were under that fig tree I saw you."

And that was too much for him. Remember, in those days there were no telephones, televisions, cameras. And so he believed. But the text that I want to give you is 1 Peter 2, because this is the context which it is used here in Revelation 14. 1 Peter 2:21-22. Now I want you at home to read the context. The context is, "We must be willing to suffer wrongfully for Christ." That's the context. Peter is admonishing the believers, "When you are mistreated, what do you do? Do you fight back? No, you must be willing to suffer wrongfully." 1 Peter 2:21:

To this you were called, because Christ suffered for you, leaving you an example, that you should follow in his steps.

Did He deserve that suffering? No. Was He willing to suffer? Yes. Why? Because He loved us. He was "leaving us an example, that we should follow in His steps." And then His steps are described in 1 Peter 2:22-23:

"He committed no sin, and no deceit was found in his mouth." When they hurled their insults at him, he did not retaliate; when he suffered, he made no threats. Instead, he entrusted himself to him who judges justly.

He did not say, "I'll get you back!" He doesn't say that. Or, "I'll take you to court!" He didn't do that. 1 Peter 2:24:

He himself bore our sins in his body on the tree, so that we might die to sins and live for righteousness; by his wounds you have been healed.

Remember, wherever you have the word, "tree," it symbolizes the curse of God. Deuteronomy says, "Cursed is the man who hangs on a tree." Deuteronomy 21:22-23:

If a man guilty of a capital offense is put to death and his body is hung on a tree, you must not leave his body on the tree overnight. Be sure to bury him that same day, because anyone who is hung on a tree is under God's curse. You must not desecrate the land the LORD your God is giving you as an inheritance.

Now please note, He was willing to suffer that we might be healed. We must be willing to suffer that He might be glorified. That is what these people are, the 144,000. Now please remember, will the 144,000 be persecuted in that great tribulation? Will they be falsely accused? Will they be mistreated? Will they be reviled? You name it, they will face it. How will they react? Like Christ did. They will keep quiet, they will not fight back. Folks, that is the power of the gospel. They have no guile in their mouth, they don't fight back, they don't retaliate. The second half of verse 5:

...They are blameless.

Here are My people who have the faith of Jesus, and who are manifesting it by keeping the commandments. Or as Revelation 19:7-8 says:

Let us rejoice and be glad and give him glory! For the wedding of the Lamb has come, and his bride has made herself ready. Fine linen, bright and clean, was given her to wear. (Fine linen stands for the righteous acts of the saints.)

Also Revelation 7:14b:

These are they who have come out of the great tribulation; they have washed their robes and made them white in the blood of the Lamb.

They are a people "who have washed their robes and made them white" and this white robe is the righteousness of Christ imparted, folks.

So here are a people who will be cleansed, who will fully reflect the character of Christ. How will this happen? By promotional programs? No. By incentives? No. But by the preaching of the Three Angels' Message, and by our response to it. And the Three Angels' Message is, in verity, Christ our righteousness.

Can you see that God has a great plan for us, for the last generation of Christians? That plan will be realized by the Three Angels' Message. That message will produce a people who will be able to stand in the great tribulation, and the second coming of Christ. Do you know that Christ, in His divinity, is a consuming fire? And do you know, that anything that is not covered by His righteousness, will be consumed at the second coming? Do you know that the believers will be able to stand that glory, not because they are good in themselves, but because they are clothed with the righteousness of Christ. And they will cry: "This is our God and our Saviour that we have been waiting for!"